Footprints of Giants

Discover & Develop Habits of Greatness

Dr. T. Ayodele Ajayi

Hi Jodie,
from One author to
another

Tai
04-09-202e

MINISTRY IN ART PUBLISHING
communicating excellence

Footprints of Giants

Discover & Develop Habits of Greatness

Copyright © December 2009 by T. Ayodele Ajayi.

Ministry In Art Publishing Ltd
email admin@ministryinart.com
www.miapublishing.com

ISBN: 978-1-907402-03-6

Cover Design: Allan Sealy

THIS BOOK WILL CHANGE YOUR LIFE!

Often when reading a book we decide to apply what we read to our lives. All too often, weeks later, we have forgotten our good intentions.

Here are six practical ways of :

TURNING GOOD INTENTIONS TO PRACTICAL HABITS:

1. USE CARDS
Write out the principles or passages you want to memorize on 3" x 5" cards and review them often.

2. MARK YOUR CALENDER
Mark your calendar/ diary or set your personal digital assistant for the time you would review your good intentions.

3. RE-READ YOUR UNDERLINES
Underline or highlight key portions of books, then re-read your underlines repeatedly.

4. WRITE SUMMARY LESSON NOTES FROM YOUR STUDY
Make summary notes from your study, then re-read them repeatedly. Store them away safely for quick access and future reference.

5. APPLY THE MATERIAL IMMEDIATELY

There is an old saying

Hear something - you forget it

See something – you remember it, and

Do something- you understand it

Apply what you learn as soon as you possibly can- it helps you understand and remember it.

6. PRIORITISE WHAT YOU WANT TO LEARN

Select 1-3 things from the book, apply them faithfully and make them a habit. Remember, every living person struggles with turning his or her good intention into habits. Using these six points will turn wishing into doing.

Adapted from Dr Bill Newman's" *Soaring with Eagles, Principles of Success" (1999) and reproduced* with the kind permission of author

FOREWORD

I have read volumes over the years; everything from endless medical texts, Christian books, magazines, bulletins, newspapers, encyclopaedia, etc. This book, 'Footprint of Giants' is one of the most comprehensive and balanced set of articles on taking giant strides into greatness I have ever come across.

It is a common life-tragedy to see men and women of incredible prophecy, potential and possibilities fail to take advantage of them. To become a giant in any profession or calling requires concrete well-defined steps, and certainly those to avoid at any cost. No one becomes a giant by chance.

True greatness is attained by informed practices; definitive habits reflected in desire, dreams, decisions and development. A lifestyle of discipline, discernment, diligence and dissemination is necessary; avoiding the demise landmines others often fall into.

Dr T Ayodele Ajayi has ingeniously put together an excellent piece of profound truth.

I recommend this book to every dreamer. Do something about 'you'. Learn the essential daily strides, mindsets, actions and decisions that will enhance your pursuit of greatness. Go for gold and do not sell your great giant destiny away through carelessness, inactivity or ignorance.

A man I barely knew sat in front of me one day. Inspired by the Holy Spirit, I gazed at him intently and said 'do not wait for greatness, take it'. Do not guess your way through life; operate through facts and figures. Acquire knowledge, be wise and plot a path into great things.

As you read this book study the pearls of knowledge and wisdom and put them into practice. I see the breaking of a new day and the dawn of a new era. Congratulations, you have encountered the keys for a brilliant future.

Dr Albert Odulele
Glory House Churches International

What other giants are saying:

This is a book that will change your life if you take it seriously. It is both motivational & inspirational.

I've had the privilege to know the author for many years. I have watched him grow and develop from adolescence to manhood. We have worked together on many projects especially for" LIBERTY – making people free." I can say that Ayodele is not only an excellent writer but a giant among men. He exemplifies everything he has written. READ this book; devour it and step into the giant mentality.

Rev Mrs Kate Jinadu,
Director and Pioneer of Liberty &
Wife of General Overseer New Covenant Church

I enjoy the privilege of having Dr T Ayodele Ajayi as my Associate Pastor at New Covenant Church Charlton over the years and can boldly say that he is a man that walks the talk.

Having read the manuscripts of this book; it is a complete step-by-step pathway to wake up the sleeping giant in you into prominence. No matter what you are going through at the moment, you can join the roll call of giants by declaring boldly that you will leave footprints of greatness.

If you have been frustrated by your dreams, ideas & visions; this book will stimulate your sleeping giant and ignite the wheels of productivity. The precepts will deal a death blow to mediocrity and set you on the path of leaving footprints of greatness after you.

Two key reasons to make this book a must read: what Dr T Ayodele Ajayi has got to say and the way he says it.

Rev Franklin 'Ranti Okunowo,
Pastor New Covenant Church (Charlton) London

I think Footprints of Giants is a great piece of work. Dr Ajayi's careful layout and succinct presentation of the pillars definitely encapsulates the entire anecdote of a person's destiny. A wise man and woman will have it handy for every human endeavour.

Rev Tayo Arowojolu,
Founding Solicitor, Tayo Arowojolu Solicitors,
London UK & President Covenant Men International, UK.
(comments from listening to audio excepts)

'Footprints of Giants' is a deep and wide resource for everyone hoping to make a success of their life and impact others. I found the book totally engaging and practical.

The diligent research that went into 'Footprints of Giants' is evident. It demonstrates that Dr Ajayi practices what he advocated in the book.

Methodologically weaving through a multi-faceted serving of academic, historical, and the biblical, I am particularly impressed with the author's painstaking effort to ensure readers are taken through a journey of self discovery to a destination of self- development. This is why I wholeheartedly recommend this book to everyone and I have no doubt that the footprints of 'Footprints of Giants' will be a signpost for many in this generation and beyond.

Atinuke Badejo
Principal Partner, Lagos Finishing School
& Editor Etiquette Bank Blog

I was privy to reading chapters of this book early in the year. It was fundamental in forming new habits and propelling me towards objectives I have struggled with in the past which I am now beginning to achieve. I am looking forward to reading the entire book in a bounded copy.

Akinwunmi Ladapo
IT Consultant & UK Liberty Travelling Team Pastor.

I am sure my daddy's book would benefit anyone who reads it.

Buyikunmi Ajayi

DEDICATION

This book is dedicated to the progressive advancement of the life transforming work Liberty is doing in unreached villages of Africa. What a delight, privilege and fulfilment to be a member of the team planting such giant and eternal footprints.

ACKNOWLEDGEMENT

One may wonder how a Psychiatrist ended up as an inspirational author. I am the first to admit and acknowledge the profound grace of God on my life to conceive, commence and complete this book.

I am highly indebted to several people that the Lord has endowed me with. My sincere thanks go to Rev and Rev Mrs Paul Jinadu who I fondly refer to as my spiritual grandparents. Mummy Kate working with you in Liberty has been a tremendous learning experience in ministry. I am also grateful to Rev Niyi Kolade for exemplary leadership in godliness, and Rev Femi Omisade for relentlessly preaching on living ones dream until I believed it enough to make a move. My appreciation also goes to my dear pastor Rev Franklin Okunowo and his dearly beloved wife Mrs Reni Okunowo for being good shepherds, supporting my dream and freely giving me a podium. Thanks to Rev Dr Albert Odulele who carried me on his shoulders for a breath taking view.

I appreciate all the members of my master mind group- Rev Gbenro Adewunmi, my twin brother Ayoola, Oluwaseun Ajayi, Oluwaseyi Oluwadare, Tosin & Yinka Akibu, Akinwunmi Ladapo and Robert Palmer. Indeed, your input made a world of difference. Also my thanks go to my other brothers and sisters for their unflinching support. I am indebted to my New Covenant Church Charlton family who have offered me the benefit of their audience and encouraging feedback for several years. I would not leave out my protégés Elizabeth & Claire Odunaike and Ayobami Salami who have embraced the message of this book on a personal note.

I value the input of Rev .Tayo Arowojolu and Mrs Atinuke Badejo for their review and the vote of confidence passed in the *Footprint of Giants* .

I am highly indebted to my parents- Daddy & Mummy Kolapo & Mercy Ajayi & my Parents-in-Love – Daddy & Mummy David & Alice Oluwadare for relentless seasons of intercession to nurture this work from conception to completion. You are the best.

Finally I owe a lot of gratitude to my precious wife, Modupe. Thank you for the countless nights you slept overnight on the living room sofa in order to be with me as I typed up the manuscripts. I appreciate your selflessness in releasing and supporting me to be the Giant I was born to be. Thank you for holding my hand, walking with me and believing in me until I emerged out of my MRCPsych. wilderness. I celebrate with you today, the wiping away of our tears.

To my two princesses Oluwabuyikunmi & Araoluwa ,who though, miss Daddy sorely when he is away visiting Nigeria for Liberty outreach, take consolation in the fact that "our Dad has gone to help children who are in need" . I'm proud of you both. You are giants in your own right.

ABOUT THE AUTHOR

Dr T. Ayodele Ajayi is a Psychiatrist and a member of the Royal College of Psychiatrists. His academic work has been published in leading national medical and psychiatric journals and cited internationally.

He is an Associate Pastor with one of the several branches of New Covenant Church in London. Ayodele is also a medical volunteer with Liberty, the charity arm of the church that works liberating communities in unreached villages of Africa by providing free education, health services, agricultural empowerment, clean water and pastoral care.

Ayodele's passion is to see everyone he encounters, particularly the youth, discover and fulfil their full destiny in Christ. He is an encourager, gifted teacher and budding Life Coach cum Youth Mentor.

He is married to Modupe and they are blessed with two gorgeous daughters.

CONTENTS

Introduction

1   Dimensions of greatness 29

2.   Deep Secret in Habits 55

3.   Desire Habits of Giants 79

4.   Decision Habits of Giants 91

5.   Development Habits of Giants. 117

6.   Discipline Habits of Giants. 139

7.   Discernment Habits of Giants 179

8.   Diligence Habits of Giants 207

9.   Dissemination of Giants 223

10. Demise of Giants 239

11. Giant of all Giants . .. .261

INTRODUCTION

All humans were born giants, many may know it, some know how to manifest greatness, few live as such, but alas; even fewer remain giants long enough to leave a mark on time! It is those even fewer lot who know they were born great; know how to unravel their greatness and go ahead to habitually practise what they know, that leave a footprint on the sand of time. They are those who set personal standards that eventually become gold standards in their fields of endeavour.

Call them giants, achievers or inventors. Others like to think of them as trial blazers, pace setters or pathfinders. Those who recognise them call them eminent, distinguished or outstanding. They are nicknamed stars, successful and sophisticated. Whatever the name you give to giants, allow me to propose to you from the outset that there is a giant in you too. There is a giant in you waiting to be unravelled. You may not be called a guru, high- flyer or authority in your endeavour yet, but I assure you were born to be great.

This book is written to show you how to add your name to that roll of honour of those who leave a lasting legacy on their world. I challenge you to add your name to that list of the distinguished champions because there is indeed a giant in you. You may not know it yet. You may not how to, you may not be living as such, but all does not negate the truth that there is a giant in you.

They are many giants walking around with bowed heads. They are living as midgets, Lilliputians and average people. Every human on earth is like a giant chest of treasures locked up by a secret code. Becoming a giant you were born to be is akin to finding and habitually using the correct code to unlock the path to greatness. Achieving greatness is not rocket science, it is about finding the code and habitually applying them each step of the way up the ladder as the treasure chest is unlocked and its content appreciated.

All humans were designed to leave a mark on time like caterpillars destined to blossom into beautifully clad butterflies. Free to fly rather than crawl and liberated from their cocoons with a mission to fly from one flower to another. We are free to pollinate the world with grace and beauty. We were born free to fly gracefully from one place to the other leaving behind a trial of colour, flavour and scent in the world and lives of those we encounter.

Indeed, there are many in the pangs and pain of unfulfilled expectation who may not know they are giants in embryo. They are those who recognise there is greatness in them but are struggling to give it expression. They realise by their instincts that there is an eagle in them but somehow they cannot quite reach the stage of soaring. They are living like the frustrated caterpillars stuck in its cocoon, akin to the disillusioned eagle trapped as an eaglet.

Benjamin Disraeli, a nineteenth century eminent British Prime Minister once said, "the greatest good you can do for others is not just to share your riches but to reveal to him his own". The famous Chinese proverb reiterates this message - "Give a man a fish and he will eat for a day. Teach a man how to fish and he will eat for a lifetime". My mandate in the *Footprint of Giants* is to show from personal experience, study and account of others that every human was born great and there is a path to greatness. Greatness has time tested and proven tracks. My aim would have been achieved if on turning the final page of this book my reader goes away with a conviction that indeed they are giants in their own rights. It is my desire to show you the paths to a life that counts by drawing analogies and showing harmony from scriptures, the secular and science.

I have found there is a striking common thread that identifies achievers. An uncanny harmony between scriptures, the secular and science asserts that greatness has tracks and is predictable. Outstanding and lasting success in any of life's endeavour, be it marriage, career, parenting, business or ministry has a traceable path that can be found and followed. The inevitable consequence of such discovery and mastery is outstanding success.

Allow me to share with you the words of an eminent God's general of our time, who by living example has demonstrated this harmony between scriptures, science and the secular. Bishop David Oyedepo of the Living faith ministries said

> *Hitherto many have thought that sense knowledge is contrary to scriptural and spiritual knowledge. But without a good sense knowledge, you can't understand the things of the spirit. Your spirit can't instruct your body, it is your mind that does that; because the body only responds to instructions from the mental region. Your spirit illuminates your mind, passing on information to it, and then your mind dispatches it to the body, for appropriate actions.*

In essence, there is a harmony between scripture, science and secular, the observance of which results in astronomical success.

Indeed, there is no new pathway to greatness other than as expressed in scriptures, affirmed by science and adopted by the secular. It is the discovery and habitual practice of those fundamental principles that result in outstanding success and greatness. The ignorance or defiance of such principles however leads to a life of misery and frustration. All caterpillars were destined to become butterflies but only if they know how. All chicken eggs designed to become full- grown chickens, but only if they endure incubation.

From personal experience and study, I have arrived at a firm conclusion that the species Homo sapiens is too heavily endowed to live casually and die without a footprint on time. If he does because of his ignorance of his distinguished status or oblivion of the path to expressing his status, it would have been the greatest tragedy of all time. Somebody ones said that the saddest words of tongue or pen are "it might have been". The tragedy of life is not that we die, but what dies inside the man while he lives (Albert Schweitzer).It is my prayer that reading this book would spare you that tragedy.

Look at the statistics and convince yourself of your uniqueness. Do you know that, though there are six billion human beings on earth, only one in about every million living organism is a human being? I hope you can conclude from these figures that indeed you are unique and great in your own right. You are not as cheap a being as you previously imagined! There would never be another you, so make the most of your life. There would never be another time so make the best of today. Remember yesterday is history tomorrow is future and today is a gift; and that is why it is called present. Now is the time to live as the giant you were born to be.

I concur with the wit who said that, "from testimonials and personal experience we have enough information to conclude that it is possible to design and live an extra ordinary life" (Jim Rohn, International entrepreneur and leading business philosopher). Life is meaningless if it is not remarkable. We will be known forever by the tracks we leave. Life is about making impact and being a blessing; leaving your world a better and richer place than it would have been without you. It is about enhancing and adding value and enriching the world and lives of its inhabitants.

I challenge you to fast -forward your imagination to what would be said at your funeral when you grow old, fulfil your years and bow off the stage of life. What would be written on your epitaph stone when your work is done in seventy, eighty or perhaps ninety years from now? What would you be remembered for? What would those whose lives you have the rare and golden opportunity to affect now say of you when the curtain of your life is drawn together?

As you contemplate these searching questions in your heart, I invite you to come with me in the adventure of looking into the bible, science and secular experiences As we trail together the footprint of giants!

It is my earnest expectation that before you finish reading this book you would decide how you wish to live. As for me, I have decided that others may live mediocre lives but not me. Others may be content to live and leave without a legacy, but not me. Others may live without a mark, but I, would live as a giant leaving footprints to follow in my time. Allow me to conclude this introductory chapter with Marianne Williamson's words "We ask ourselves who am I to be brilliant, gorgeous, talented and rich? Actually, who are you not to be? Your playing small doesn't serve the world". And may I then add, so rise up, and embrace greatness.

⁕

CHAPTER 1

Dimensions of Greatness

Start with the end in mind! So says Stephen Covey, bestselling author of *Habits of Highly Effective People*.

If we must live as giants, a good place to start would be to know who giants are. Are they born or made? Can all individuals become giants? What allows an ordinary everyday person to manifest greatness and live an extraordinary life? What are the secrets of giants? How do giants maintain their status?

As one embarks on trailing the footprint of giants these questions become relevant. We must know who are a giant is first before we decide we would like to be one. Before we begin to trail their footprints we need to ensure where it leads is where we wish to go. Allow me to present the credentials of the giant before we travel far in our trailing journey.

The giant whose path we attempt to trail is that person who recognises that every human being is a unique miracle, themselves not the least. They know no one on earth was born without a mission. They recognise they have great potential, latent power enough to fulfil their life's work. Enough is hidden in them to influence their world and make it a better place than they met it. Our distinguished person knows they were born for great things and know how to achieve these things.

This enlightened person has discerned that greatness is in service. Giants recognise that the rung on the ladder of greatness are lined with the towel of service. They recognise whom they were born to serve. They know what their life's mission is, and they are busy living every day walking towards that Golden Fleece. The star we describe recognises that greatness is not in talk or wishful dreams. Rather it is in a firm decision to accomplish a clear dream accompanied by habitual steps of right actions that produce greatness. They talk the talk but also walk the walk. This person knows it is more important to walk the walk than talk the talk.

They realise you cannot reach the distant beautiful island until you first leave the comfort and security of the shore. The person we speak of has left the "some-day island" and boarded the ship named *action* cruising towards the sunnier climes of glory land. Giants recognise there is more to life than building a little empire surnamed "ME"! They are too busy building a paradise for those to whom they have a mission, than to be preoccupied with their own palaces.

Our giant is not primarily motivated by money or personal gain, but by how money can perpetually transform the lives of those they serve. They are driven by what they can give rather than what they can get. They, like John F. Kennedy proposed in his presidential inauguration speech, are no longer asking what their nation can do for them but what they can do for their nation.

The giant is the person who devotes his life to raising orphans in low- income areas of Asia by building orphanages. They think of the disadvantaged youth from the villages of Africa who has wits but lacks opportunity, and they respond to their inner nudging to establish scholarship schemes. How about the one whose life's dream is to see homeless drug addicts in the ghettos of New York completely rehabilitated and reintegrated into society. He is driven by a passion to see each addict break the restricting clutch of the "next fix" and librated into a world in which he is an asset to his community. Our exceptional person reads in the national news the disheartening figures that teenage pregnancy in United Kingdom ranks top of the league in Europe and they begin a school based teenage lady's virtue club to combat the menace. The liberality with which abortion is accepted in the society bothers them enough to devote their life to raising awareness on the ethical and moral evil in the issue. Their heart bleeds enough to take action about the gun crime that has become a commonplace among our youngsters. They start a neighbourhood "No weapons" club in their community. Our man or woman is one who sees a need in the society that grieves their heart enough to action rather than moan and grip.

Our prodigious person does not have to take on a course of national or global impact to be a giant. She could be the single mother of three down the street who has decided come what may, her children would turn out into respectable members of the community who will in turn become eminent in their own right. The story of the illiterate mother of Dr Ben Carson, world leading Paediatrician Neurosurgeon comes to mind. Dr Carson was inducted into the Academy of Achievement in 1995. According to citation on their website it was Mrs Sonya Carson who raised Benjamin and his brother single-handed after her divorce when he was only eight. Sonya supported her son to rise from bottom to the top of his fifth grade class by restricting access to television and outdoor play time. These treats were subject to satisfactory completion of home work and writing a report on two library books he was required to read each week.

Mrs Carson's diligent parenting paid off when Benjamin quickly rose to the top of his class. She had ignited in him a quest for knowledge which served him in subsequent years of his career. He went on to graduate with honours from high school, completed a degree in Psychology from the ivy league Yale University before studying Medicine in Michigan University.

Carson went on to complete a Neurosurgical residency at the reputable John Hopkins Hospital in Baltimore, and by age thirty –two accomplished the feat of becoming the Hospital's Director of Paediatric Neurosurgery. He added even more feathers to his cap and made medical history, when in 1987 he led a team of seventy in a twenty two hour successful surgical separation of the Binder Siamese twins. There was no precedence to this successful separation of twins joined at the back of their heads.

Mrs Carson's story demonstrates that the giant is not necessarily the top man in his organisation. He may not be the pastor of his church or the director of the company. He is however that man or woman who has found and fitted perfectly doing their bit where they belong in the organisation and society. She is that usher in the congregation who gives everyone who walks through the door a million pound red carpet welcome each time she is at her duty post. She is not interested in whether the pastor is looking or not, she just gets on with the job. She does not make light her role and considers it as important as the role of the pastor who preaches the message.

The giant here is the solicitor's office junior clerk who though is currently ranked low on the organisation's personnel chart recognises he plays a crucial role. He does not allow contempt of his current apparently menial role to undermine his productivity and commitment. He realises that as long as he is faithful and contentious in his current post, the only medium that separates him from the top position is time.

Our person of the moment is no fool or blind optimist. They not only know they are destined for great things but also recognise there is a price of habitually walking in what they know in order to become who they wish to be. The price in developing their potential, being disciplined in their appetites and diligent in their endeavours is a reality to these rare breeds. These folks have rightly discerned their own worth to the world and have decided they are not here to while away time or play games with life. They have a mission to accomplish and they do not intend to exit without living out their full potential. These folks do not wait long for opportunity to turn up before creating one to serve those to whom they have a mission.

Our champions are those who realise that life is a marathon not a sprint. They have set out on their life's goal adopting a long- term view. They do not intend to be stars one moment and by the next become a byword of faded glory whilst they are yet alive. They have factored in staying power into their race. These folks realise it takes as much if not more effort to sustain than achieve greatness. They intend to continue to live optimally productive lives in their senior years having spent their early and middle years replicating in others their good virtues. By such a stance, they would have succeeded in multiplying their output in an astronomical fashion.

The people we are about to trail belong to the stock of those who are themselves seasoned trailers of other giants who have gone ahead of them. They not only reproduce but also resonate. They realise the path to greatness is expressly laid out, if only we search well enough. They find for themselves those who have been to where they are headed and follow their every word, advice and habit closely. We can learn from them that you really do not need to re invent the wheel. The ageless principles and values that is crucial to leading a life that counts have remained few and unchanged over the generations. All one needs to do is to find and practise them. Then, and only then can the inevitable destination be, becoming the giant one was always destined to be.

Let us now examine what Jesus; the giant of all giants had to say to His followers about greatness and giants

Giants are Servants

Mark 10:42-45

But Jesus called to them to himself and said to them" You know that those who are considered rulers over the Gentiles lord it over them, and their great ones exercise authority over them.

Yet it shall not be so among you; but whoever desires to be great among you shall be your servant.

And whoever of you desires to be first shall be slave of all.

For even the Son of Man did not come to be served, but to serve and to give his life a ransom for many".

The path to greatness is very clearly delineated in these scriptures as service to others. The way up is down and there are no short cuts. If you want to be a giant, discover those, to whom you have been sent, find them and get lost in serving them. Go out and find them wherever they may be-the leper's colony in India, the delinquent youth in Europe, the widows in Africa; find them and serve them! Promotion automatically pursues diligent service as a matter of course. The path to greatest is not in the number of titles or degrees one amasses. The greatest is not the one who exerts and parades themselves as the boss. Rather greatness is a function of the quality service you render in your appointed duty post.

Let us conclude this chapter by confirming from scriptures previously made assertions

Every human was born great

Psalms 139:13-15

For you did form my inward parts; you did knit me together in my mother's womb.

I will confess and praise you for you are fearful and wonderful and for the awful wonder of my birth! Wonderful are your works, and that my inner self knows very well.

My frame was not hidden from you when I was being formed in secret and intricately and curiously wrought [as if embroidered with various colours] in the depths of the earth [a region of darkness and mystery]

These verses describe as intricate and careful, the process in which humans are made. Wrought curiously and created scrupulously in a fit- for -purpose fashion. Every human is a miracle and we must all live life with a sense of purpose cherishing the gift of today.

Every human was born with a mission & potential to accomplish them

There is enough evidence in scriptures showing that all humans have a pre- destined mission on earth.

Jeremiah1:5.

"Before I formed thee in the belly, I knew thee, and before thou came forth out of the womb, I sanctified thee and I ordained thee a prophet to the nations".

These were God's reassuring word's to Prophet Jeremiah that he had a pre-determined mission before he was created, and he was fashioned and equipped to fulfil these mission.

No matter how beyond your natural ability your life mission may appear at the outset, I am glad to bear good news that it can be accomplished. You have all it requires to run and finish your race. Don't buckle under the weight or throw in your towel in acceptance of defeat!

Read another reassuring verse of scripture with the same message

Ephesians2:10 Amp

"For we are God's (own) handiwork (His workmanship), recreated in Christ Jesus (born anew)that we may do those good works, which God predestined (planned beforehand)for us(taking paths which he prepared ahead of time), that we should walk in them(living the good life which He prearranged and made ready for us to live".

This one needs no further interpretation as it speaks for itself. You have been designed and fitted for your life's mission. This mission was already in God (your creator's) heart before you were ever conceived in your mother's womb. Your role is to find the pre determined purpose and begin to walk in it. Only then can you live the good life He prepared for you ahead of time. When that purpose is not found or embraced life becomes monotonous, uneventful and difficult. If your life currently lacks lustre and positive adventure, could it be because you are yet to find and embrace your life's mission? Life on the path to greatness is exciting even at challenging twists and turns.

Allow me to share with you a few fundamental truths about the dimensions of greatness.

Dimension of Individuality

Contrary to what many believe and live by, the race to greatness is an individual one. It is a race against oneself and the divinely predetermined *good work* rather than a race against the neighbour down the road or work colleague. It is a race against time to run your pre- allotted race and finish being optimally accomplished.

This insight that the journey to becoming a giant is person specific according to God's plan liberates from the rat race of wanting to outsmart the other colleague, businessperson or pastor across the road. It delivers from the temptation to be jealous and envious of the success of another. I have my own territory in life and if I find it and excel there, I would have no need to be envious of others who are equally excelling in their own territory. If you feel intimidated by the success story and achievement of others, it could be because you are yet to find and excel in your own domain.

All of us are kings but we must first find our kingdoms in order to reign. Your kingdom is those to whom you were sent. It is in the process of serving them that you reign. When you find your kingdom and serve in it reigning would no longer be a chore but a course.

The person whose *good work* is to remain a faithful business entrepreneur generating finance to build orphanages, sink wells, and set up Well Women Clinics in less developed areas of the globe; would not be deemed a giant if they abandoned this *good work* to build a "successful" mega church or become lost in a self aggrandizement pursuit of academia.

No human can experience genuine, fulfilling and lasting success except when in the centre of divine will. No one can swim against the tide of his pre-determined purpose and arrive accomplished. Can you imagine attempting to swim up the Niagara Falls? Much precious time, resources and effort would be preserved when one finds what God's yardstick of greatness is and then sets out to meet that standard. Do yourself the lifetime favour of finding what your life's mission is and when you do, stick to it and serve those to whom you were called. Stop the trial and error game. A rolling stone gathers no moss!

Dimension of Time

Becoming a giant is a process not an event. I like the way Mr Denis Waitley, internationally renowned Olympic performance coach puts it-"success is a process that continues, not a status that you reach. If you are alive there are lessons to be learned".

The beauty in achieving is not always restricted to goal realisation but also in what you become in the process of achieving. The process of time allows to mature in the pursuer virtues that otherwise would not have developed. Time is a crucial and inevitable factor in the journey to prominence and significance. If you wish to live a life that counts, then be prepared to allow for the transforming influence of experience. Experience comes with time. View life as a marathon not a hundred metres dash!

The great book says

"To everything there is a season and a time to every purpose under heaven". (Ecclesiastes 3:1).

It takes time to achieve greatness and become a giant. The same master who appointed the mission (good work) also has a calendar and agenda. There is a right time and season for your life's purpose and mission. The phases appear to follow the progression as thus.

Phase of ignorance

There is a time of ignorance when humans are oblivious that they have been born to fulfil a mission. This is the time of careless bliss when divine purpose has not been perceived. This is not a zone to spend a significant part of one's life without consequence. It is better used as a transition to further dimensions down the path of greatness. I pray that if anyone reading this book be in such a state of ignorance, there would have been a positive transition by the time you complete this book.

Phase of restlessness

The apparent bliss of ignorance is followed by a period of restlessness and dissatisfaction. Somewhere deep down in your heart you realise that there is more to your life than what currently exists.

You may be on your job and you cannot get over the thought of reaching for something better and beyond as you commute to work daily. I recount listening to the story of a man who worked as a station assistant for the London underground but knew deep in his heart he was on the wrong job. He would not accept his employer's proposal to apply for a higher position because he knew his future and greatness lay elsewhere. He eventually left his underground post in a phased manner after developing his bespoke haberdashery business by the side. Today this accomplished gentleman finds satisfaction in not only making bespoke suits for the noble but also representing them as councillor in his local council. This, he would not have been able to achieve without the state of restlessness which led to resigning his underground position.

Perhaps you can identify with the story you have just read. You feel like a woman in the pangs of labour who is about to birth a new life. I invite you to consider the next dimension of timing.

Phase of searching

This is a period in which restlessness is intense enough to provoke a quest for insight. It is a period of studying, prayerful searching, and counsel seeking. A time when the heart seeks to know the mission one was made to fulfil on earth. It is a period of asking deep soul- searching questions with an expectation for answers. I am glad to bear good news that *"You will seek Me and find Me when you search for Me with all your heart"* (Jeremiah 29:13 New American standard version). Every genuine and ardent seeker is guaranteed finding.

The period of seeking often entails periods of solitude and separation from the luxuries of life. Many times the secret of one's life's work is revealed not in the pleasurable atmosphere of the palace but in the painful terrains of the desert.

Phase of revelation

Thankfully, the relentless seekers are guaranteed finding. Indeed, there comes a time when the revelation of what one's life mission is, begins to unfold in phases. Many times the big picture or end product is revealed at the outset, but the stages, steps and methods to arrive at the destination is revealed in phases at a time. It is my experience and those of others I have studied that further revelation only usually follows action on previous revelation. As you begin to act on the current nudging in your heart, the path to greatness becomes better illuminated. Have you taken action yet on what you already know you need to do? If you have not, then you should not really expect further light on your journey.

Phase of pursuit

The time of revelation should be followed by the time of pursuit. If you already know to whom you were called to serve, embark on the journey to greatness by pursuit of your course. The first step in pursuit is preparation. Find out what you already have and what you need to have, become or acquire to reach your destination.

Preparation usually entails development. It may mean private study, formal study, tutelage or even voluntary service. Whatever it is that you find you need to do to prepare for your journey, spare no time, expense or resources in acquiring them. It may entail learning a new skill or polishing your talents and abilities.

May I warn that your current job, position or title may have no direct bearing whatsoever to your life's mission? You may however acquire basic life skills and lessons from any job you hold. If you must become a giant, you must be willing to trade your current apparently secure position for a land of the unknown and uncharted.

I also find that God arranges by divine providence to bring into your life and path experiences and people who are crucial to your journey during the phase of preparation and pursuit. Stop weeping and moaning about your boss, he may as well be one of those crucial to your reaching greatness and becoming a giant. You may need the skills you are acquiring on that job you so despise now, in order to get to the place of your greatness.

May I advice you that if you have found your mission embrace it as your path to greatness and follow it with passion. Endeavour to take an action each day, no matter how small to move you towards the ultimate goal.

The phase of preparation is followed by pursuit. Do not hang around waiting for the time to pursue the dreams you have etched on your heart. Step out and step up. Until you do so you may not see events unfold. I like the way a wit once put it -"If I hadn't believed it, I wouldn't have seen it". You may not see any tangible evidence that you are pursuing greatness until you step out in faith and back your persuasion with relevant positive action.

There is no short cut to these phases in the timing dimension of greatness. You are not allowed to cut corners. There are no sudden get- rich- quick schemes in divine agenda. No sudden ministry explosions without preceding unknown periods of little but faithful beginnings. I always marvel when I see folks who hop from one anointing service to the other seeking anointing exclusively by the laying on of hands.

I am a firm believer in impartation by laying of hands, but I have also come to realise that it takes more than hand laying to carry a sustained unction of God on one's life. There is an anointing that can only be acquired from habitual meaningful fellowship with Christ (the anointed one) Himself. One could not agree more with Rev George Adegboye, a dear father in the faith who once said "the unction of the spirit is not learnt. It is something you earn on your knees". I concur!

Be it in building of character, ministry, marriage or career, God's sure pattern is to transform from glory to glory; and from strength to strength. He never deals in microwave successes or quick fixes. Avoid and resist the temptation of cutting corners to arrive at a sudden success. It never lasts and the path is froth with heartaches and disasters.

Phase of accomplishment

Contrary to what the twenty first century media propagate, dreams do come true. In truth, there is a period of accomplishment when the dreams, which had for many years resided in the recesses of human hearts, becomes tangible and palpable. This is an encouraging word to everyone who is about to give up on that dream because of delays and detours in the journey. Hang in there, dreams do come true. It may just be round the corner for you.

The period of accomplishment is indeed one of satisfaction and fulfilment. It is a time of celebration, but not one for complacency. It is crucial to realise that success can be the trigger or catalyst to astronomical failure when poorly managed. If the status of greatness is to endure, the period of accomplishment must be used to forge and explore newer frontiers of greatness.

I once read a fascinating yet revealing piece of history about the Roman Empire. Aristotle in his *Politics* told of how the proud and powerful Spartans "remained secure as long as they were at war" and then "collapsed as soon as they acquired an empire". They did not know how to use the leisure that peace brought. If you are in the phase of accomplishment, what steps are you taking to ensure it is an enduring phase? What actions are you taking to guard against complacency and decay?

Dimension of Choice

Intriguingly, greatness has always been the consequence of choice rather than chance. The responsibility for unravelling inherent greatness or otherwise has been handed to humans. The choice to succeed is one God has given to every person to make. If anyone achieves greatness in any endeavour of life, it is always because they make a choice rather than sit around for chance. It is only by choice and not chances that chains of mediocrity are broken. There is no such thing as greatness by chance or luck .Such stories are exclusively limited to the pages of fairy tale novels and they never exist in reality.

If you must become a giant, then it would be the result of choosing where you wish to go and taking appropriate steps to reach your destination. You make your choices and your choices make you. Your current level of greatness is a function of your past choices. Your future level of greatness is a product of present choices. So watch the choices you are making and do not leave your future to chance.

Once your decision takes you over it would etch in your heart a dream that results in relentless pursuit. It is only when a habit is made of relentless pursuit by positive action and patience that greatness is achieved. Should greatness ever be achieved by chance, it would be of limited impact and would not endure. There is a choice to be made in a man's thought, talk and task if he is to succeed. The habit of the choice making process determines eventual outcome.

Never believe anyone who says they became a champion by being lucky. Stars are made not by wishing or waiting but by working. I would rather believe the wise man who said *"the harder you work the luckier you get."*

No man can make the choice to become a giant for you. You have to make a personal decision, find your own mission, dream your own dreams and follow them on the path of greatness to accomplishment. Greatness is not and can never be a passive process. There are no daydreamers in the league of giants. There are only dreamers who wake up, get dressed and take action on their dreams. They engage in consistent, relevant, commensurate action long enough to see their dreams unfold.

Let us conclude this chapter by describing another crucial hallmark of giants. In fact, it is this hallmark that this book centres on. It is the habits of giants. It is their habits, born out of consistent, repeated actions that giants are known by. It is their habits that they leave as footprints on the sand of time for others to follow. Habits are the paths that giants wear in the sod of time by a repetitive pattern of right thought and action.

William Arthur Ward once said "our words reveal our thoughts, our manners mirror our self-esteem, our actions reflect our character, our habits predict the future." It is your present habits that predict your future. It is your present habits that you would be remembered by. Calmness, haughtiness, justice, forthrightness are all virtues or vices of habit. If indeed you wish to go far, far enough to arrive at your life's destination, you must mind your habits. You make your habits initially, but eventually they make you!

Chapter One summary

1. One who desires to be a giant must start off by recognising who a giant is.

2. Giants recognise that every human being is unique and created with a life mission and inherently endowed to fulfil that mission.

3. Giants recognise that greatness is hidden in service. They recognise who they were called to serve and they have made decisions to live habitually taking conscious steps towards fulfilling their dreams.

4. Giants take positive action even when it hurts. They are more preoccupied with building a paradise for others than a palace for themselves. They are not motivated by money but how it can transform their served community.

5. Giants meet rather than moan about needs in their vicinity. They are not necessarily the top man in their organisation, but they optimally play their part wherever they are.

6. Giants are not blind optimists. They recognise manifesting greatness takes discipline and diligence. They take life seriously enough to create opportunities for service if none comes along.

7. Giants adopt a long -term view to life. They take steps to ensure they remain fruitful even in their latter years.

8. Giants are not only motivators for greatness but also imitators of other giants.

9. Jesus, the greatest giant of all, taught His followers that anyone who desires greatness must first be a servant.

10. The bible teaches that

   Every human was uniquely made by God in a fit for purpose fashion.

   All humans were born with a life's mission and ability

We are not enslaved by good habits, but rather might it be said that no man is truly free to advance and to make rapid progress till he has succeeded in establishing a mass of useful habits.

Walter Dill Scott

We are what we repeatedly do. Excellence then, is not an act, but a habit.

Aristotle

CHAPTER 2

Deep Secret in Habits.

How intriguing is the fact that the homeless person on the street and the Director in charge in the boardroom has but the same quantity of resource endowed daily upon them. The Pastor of the mega church and the one down the road who is struggling to break even has the same quantity of the natural endowment I speak of. The salesman who has won the salesman of the year award for the last 5 years in a row and the one who is barely holding on to his job due to under performance both have daily equal allotment of the commodity I refer to. The difference in management of that common endowment is what explains the difference between these two examples of men at extreme poles of the achievement spectrum.

Every human on earth can be outstanding at what they do if they learn to manage their resource optimally. Manifesting greatness then sounds so simplistic if one can correctly identify what this natural endowment is and how to manage it optimally. Every living human is naturally endowed with sixty seconds every minute, sixty minutes every hour, twenty four hours daily, one hundred and sixty eight hours weekly and at least seven hundred and twenty hours monthly. It is what one does with those hours, which account for where one ends up. However, the manner in which each of those individual minutes is spent matters much less than the recurring pattern of how the hours, days and months are spent. Whatever reveals the recurring style of spending time reveals the clue to whether success is inevitable or not. The secret clue is in the habitual use of time. The pattern or recurring style of time use is formed from the way we choose to use time over and again until it results in a habit that is hard to break. That habit is what holds a clue to whether we succeed or fail in our life's endeavour. Human habits are one of the most profound predictors of the outcome in the future.

The secret to greatness in all of life's pursuits and endeavours; be it marriage, ministry, career, business, parenting or sports; lays hidden in daily habits. Successful outcome or otherwise is not so difficult to predict when the daily habits are carefully observed.

Human daily habits are like seeds sown into the fertile garden of life. The garden would eventually yield the fruits of the seed sown. The person who for instance habitually sows seeds of reckless and thoughtless spending cannot and should not expect to reap a financially prosperous future. The student who habitually spends their time at all night parties with little attention to their studies should expect to reap the harvest of failure in their courses. The husband who perpetually neglects his wife's emotional and physical needs and treats her cruelly should expect dividends of an unhappy marriage.

Bankruptcy, moral scandals, divorce, rebellious children, business failures and heart attacks are never sudden events. They are usually the results of simple, may be subtle, errors of judgement albeit regular. These habitual errors eventually culminate in the big event. In the converse, financial independence, a successful business empire or a marriage with Godly well-mannered children are always the result of conscious carefully worked out plans firmly based on supporting habits practiced over a long period.

The current state of greatness or otherwise reflects a harvest of previously sown seeds of habit. The popular slogan "if you don't like the crop you are reaping, check the seed you are sowing" rings true. Brian Tracey, International motivational speaker and time management guru in his book *Eat that* Frog, cautioned that ninety five percent of success in life and work will be determined by the kind of habits one develop over time. In the real sense of the phrase, there is no such thing as "innocuous habits" because habits always have consequences one way or another.

The first lesson in the path to greatness is Mind your habits! Hidden in them is the blueprint to your future.

What are habits?

A habit, by definition, is an acquired pattern of behaviour that has become almost involuntary as a result of frequent repetition.

Walter Dill Scott an eminent business psychologist defined habits as "but ways of thinking and acting which by reason of frequent repetition have become more or less automatic". This concise definition suggests that habits are the results of a learning process occurring from repetitive and frequent experiences. On the premise of Scott's definition one can safely conclude that habits are fairly permanent patterns which can however be learnt (formed) and unlearnt (broken).

A simple illustration of habit formation is in the learning of fresh driving habits to conform to the norms and standards of the new country or region of the driver. Drivers from African and American Continents who begin to drive in the United Kingdom initially find the left sided driving awkward but with practice adapt to their new environment. On the same note, licensed drivers from other countries may find themselves having to break old habits and form new ones, if they want to successfully obtain a United Kingdom drivers License. This simple illustrations emphasis that habits can be formed and broken if the required action or thought is repeated frequently enough.

Psychology and science of habit formation

Psychologists perceive habits as a mental connection that is made between something that happens (the stimulus) and the repetitive automatic reaction to it (the response). The repetition of this connection between an event and human response over a period of time is how psychologists believe habits are formed and become entrenched. In lay terms, habits are formed when the same response is applied to a similar event on a recurrent basis.

A simple illustration is forming a habit of rising early. Initially when one decides to rise from bed an hour earlier than previously, it may require the use of an alarm clock in addition to actually making yourself rise off the bed when the bell goes. However, over time the alarm becomes internal as the body and mind are programmed into the habit of rising at that same time. It is not unusual to observe that even without an alarm one habitually wakes up at the pre- programmed time. This simple illustration shows how a habit is formed as a result of the repeated similar response (rising from bed) to an event (the alarm bell).In the same token greatness is the inevitable result of habitually living by certain principles. The good news is that habits for greatness can be discovered and developed like any other habits.

It is also believed that the individual decisions we make as humans are linked to our habits by this event-reaction connection. This is a crucial fact as the decisions we make everyday of our lives is what determines whether we are travelling towards or away from greatness. Our individual decision in response to events in life is what determines whether we end up in misery or mastery.

The event-reaction theory of habit formation is founded on the understanding of a certain unique feature of the human brain. This unique feature is the brain's ability to initially resist a change in form but then retain that changed form once it has been impressed by effort or force. In lay terms, the brain would maintain its structural and chemical form even in the face of efforts or force to change it. However, after repeated consistent exposure to this effort or force, the structural and chemical features change and remain changed until another force or effort is applied. Certain structural and chemical changes occur in the cells of the human brain when it is repeatedly exposed to the same thought or action. This is usually after an initial period of resistance has been overcome.

This feature of the brain is termed plasticity by scientists. Plasticity is best illustrated using a piece of paper. A piece of paper is plastic because it would usually resist a change in form, however once the change is impressed upon it by exerting some pressure the resulting crease becomes an indelible mark. The preserved crease becomes a point of weakness for subsequent folding or bending to occur. Similarly, in the brain, each thought and action result in structural and chemical changes akin to creating a paper crease which make it easier for the brain to support a similar pattern of thought or action subsequently.

The repetition of thought or action that results in habit formation can also be illustrated by the manner in which repeated walking over the same place in a lawn wears a path in the sod. The repetition of the same chemical process and pathways by recurring actions and responses wears a groove in the brain in a manner similar to the footprints in the sod.

The plasticity principle explains why habits are automatic and the difficulty in forming new habits or overcoming old ones. It explains why a person suffering from a heart condition continues to smoke cigarettes even when the bill boards boldly caution regarding associated grave health risks of smoking. Such understanding of brain chemistry would explain die- hard nature of habits of slothfulness, poor time and money management despite the perpetrators knowledge of their onerous effects on well being. On the converse and positive note the brains plasticity also supports why good habits of honesty, healthy work ethics and diligence persist despite the sacrifice associated with them.

The take home message is that decisions are mostly the result of habits. Habits are formed after chemical and structural changes occur in the brain following an initial period of resistance. However once these changes are enforced by repeated action or thought it becomes easy and almost automatic for the habits to be maintained.

This is great news for the aspiring giant. Habits that unravel greatness can be discovered and diligently practiced until inherent greatness evolves. May I ask you what path your current habits are leading you-unto greatness or the gutter? Are your current habits the product of chance or your choice? Have you sat down to think of how they may affect your future?

The first step in changing negative habits is to discover them.

Identifying negative habits

Orison Sweet Marden said the beginning of a habit is like an invisible thread, but every time we repeat the act we strengthen the strand, add to it another filament until it becomes a great cable and binds us irrevocably in thought and act.

Habits irrespective of their positive or negative impact are usually insidious and subtle in the process of formation. Thereafter they become so automatic that it is usually difficult to recognise them and their impact in influencing the present and more importantly the future. Somebody described them as cobwebs which when fully formed become cables, which over time could become shackles of imprisonment or succours of liberation. The first step towards breaking the limiting power of a negative habit lies in identifying the habit.

Since habits are so insidious and automatic, there is much to gain by adopting a proactive scrutinising approach. Allow me to share a few recommendations on how to identify disabling habits

1. Ask God

Psalms 26:1-
Search me o Lord and try my reins.

God is the revealer of all truth and there is nothing hidden before Him. In fact, He delights in revealing the secret things to His Children .His children should therefore be confident about approaching Him to expose secret faults particularly when there are areas of unexplained failures. Many times the secret to failure in life's endeavours lies hidden in unproductive, yet obscure habits, which only God can reveal and expose.

I challenge you to get naked with God and ask him to reveal to you the habits, which inhibit you from manifesting greatness.

2. Enlist Help Of Trusted People

The folly of Moses in attempting to judge the multitude of Israelites single- handed was revealed by Jethro his heathen father –in- law. Sometimes God uses men whom He gives discernment about others habits to allow His children identify and deal with habits, which inhibit greatness. It is a profitable practice to regularly ask important people- spouses, mentors, trusted friends, bosses and spiritual leaders whom God has placed in ones life about hindering habits they may have identified which may otherwise go unnoticed.

I learnt a valuable lesson a while ago when contrary to my self -perception, my wife lovingly pointed out how I sometimes miss opportunities of obtaining vital information in conversations because of my habit of giving an opinion too quickly. Until then, I prided myself on being a careful and perceptive listener. A careful self observation of my conversational habits however disappointingly revealed I indeed over rated my skills and needed to do more listening than talking. A conscious effort to change this hasty speaking has richly enhanced my conversational skills. I am grateful for such correcting relationships in my life.

The secret of benefitting from such relationships and candid comments lies in being teachable enough to embrace correction. Do you have people in your life who can speak to you or you are a law unto yourself? No one who is too great as to humble themselves to learn from others ever remains great for long enough to leave a mark on time. It is a privilege to have people in your life who can point out your obscure unproductive habits. It is however up to you to either believe or belittle their input.

I was intrigued to read from Rev Mike Murdock's book, *The Assignment*, that he sometimes withholds correction from his subordinates when he perceives they were not ready to receive it yet. Invariably such subordinates fail to benefit from his wealth of experience in life and ministry. The loss of failing to benefit from such a man so heavily endowed with wisdom for living is unquantifiable.

Anyone who wishes to be great must imbibe an attitude that welcomes constructive criticisms. Giants in every sphere of life are not ashamed to acknowledge when they are wrong. They however, would become ashamed when they fail to change after their wrong is pointed out. If you want to go far in life, learn to embrace and benefit from criticism rather than discard every corrective comment as malicious.

3. Enlist Professional Help

The assistance and support of objective professionals is sometimes required in identifying greatness-hindering habits. For instance, the services of a competent financial adviser may be required to identify unhealthy spending habits.

I read with disappointment but concordance in *The Millionaire Next Door* the outcome of a land breaking American survey showing that high flying professionals, prominent among them physicians were the least likely to take good care of their money. They are too busy working to earn fat salaries but without time to look after their resource and nurture its growth. Hence, their net worth grossly falls short of their annual remuneration. One of the reasons cited for this short fall was that such highflying professionals tend to succumb to society's demand to live a larger than life out- to –impress life style. Another reason cited is their tendency to spend disproportionate time earning money at the detriment of looking after their hard -earned income.

This group are called the "big hat no cattle "in the Texan ranch state. Are you a big- hat- no -cattle? Do you need to enlist professional help to discover and destroy limiting habits that prevent you from playing in the league of the great?

Doctors in postgraduate training are frequently encouraged by trainers to video record several life consultations for constructive review. This exercise, albeit threatening allows candidates gain better insight into their own bedside manners and habits. The candidates are encouraged to play back sessions before varying audiences of colleagues for constructive criticism. I propose the same technique can be used by preachers, teachers, public speakers, salespeople and even parents. The league of the great is only open to those who are great enough to admit they need to learn from those greater than them.

4. Observe Patterns

Patterns of negative habits that result in failure to achieve greatness can be identified with some self-scrutiny. If there is an area in which one has persistently experienced failure or less success than anticipated, it is important to carefully observe ones habit in those areas.

It sometimes requires keeping objective records such as a weekly menu, time diaries or even spending records to identify patterns. A poor eating or time management habit may not be apparent until a carefully kept weekly log of time use and diet is observed. The resulting insight is always worth the exercise.

5. Acceptance

Identifying an unhelpful habit takes courage to accept what is revealed and set out a plan to address the problem. Making excuses for habits that hinder greatness is an easy but potentially damaging way to cop out of facing responsibility for personal success. Giants are those who are able to identify, accept and change habits that limit their pursuits.

French classical writer Francios La Rochefoucauld said" Almost all our faults are more pardonable than the methods we think up to hide them". What excuses do you make to adorn your success-jeopardising habits making them more acceptable to yourself and others? If you were offered those same excuses you offer yourself, would you buy them?

Remember that at the end of the day, becoming a giant is not a race against another but against ones own potential and divine mandate. At the bottom line if there is anyone who is being deceived by the lame excuses, it is likely to be none other, but you.

Gilbert Arland's summarises this message succinctly when he said- *When an archer misses the mark he turns and looks for fault within himself. Failure to hit the bull's eye is never the fault of the target. To improve your aim, improve yourself.*

6. Develop an action plan

Giants are people who have the courage not only for self -scrutiny but to follow the process through with action to rectify flaws. The benefits of introspection is realised only when a carefully designed plan to alter outcome is followed through. Are you ready to boldly face the limiting habits in your life and devise a plan to address them? Until you reach this stage, greatness may remain a desirable but unachieved status.

Forming New Habits

The essence of identifying habits that stifle and inhibit greatness is to replace them with success promoting habits. Much has been said and written about how to form new habits. My personal experience and knowledge of literature can be summarized as thus

1. Be Realistic

It is reasonable and pragmatic to set out working on forming one new habit at a time. Great people are aware that an over ambitious approach to forming pro success habits inevitably becomes counter productive. Setting out to wake up an hour earlier, work an hour later and commence an exercise program all at once is less likely to be achieved than focussing on one of these goals over pre -determined period.

2. Be Committed

Commitment to forming pro greatness habits can be demonstrated in a number of ways. Giants demonstrate their commitment to change by being specific enough to write down what they commit to change. Thinking on paper has a dual advantage of clarifying thoughts and entrenching a commitment that is beyond the level of mere thoughts without corresponding action.

Commitment is also demonstrated in being accountable to others in following a habit through. The ultimate commitment however is to God and oneself. This book may never have gone pass the light bulb moment of conception, but for the announcement of my commitment to my wife within hours of its conception.

3. Be Consistent

The bare truth is forming a new habit, particularly ones that promote greatness, is not a task for the wavering person. It is however achievable. The scientific knowledge available on habit formation propounds that it is a repeated action or thought that results in overcoming the brains inherent resilience to change. Olympic champions speak plainly about the challenge of keeping to a consistent program of training to achieve desirable outcomes. Each of them sticks to the programme, form the habit and reap the dividend at the winners stand.

Rising early, studying daily, cultivating healthy eating, money and time management are habits that take a consistent approach to achieve. Most studies show that it takes three to four weeks of daily practice before any habit becomes entrenched. Great people realise the secret of repeating the same difficult pattern until it becomes an automatic, effortless enjoyable habit. They realise it is better to limit your early morning daily exercise time on a day you are running late for work rather than to cop out and forgo the exercise completely for that day.

4. Be Courageous

Giants have the courage to continue in the pursuit of healthy habits even in the face of negating circumstances. You can expect that it would rain overnight lowering temperatures to freezing cold on the morning you resolve to start getting up an hour earlier to pray and study the scriptures.

The difference between giants and failures is that great people use the excuses as the reason to carry on whilst failures use them as a reason not to. Be courageous in the face of hostile and negating circumstances that threaten to side -track you in your pursuit of greatness. It is helpful to know that any pursuit worth more than a transient passing value would face opposition. Unfortunately, many pursuers misinterpret the fierce opposition as a warning for an unfruitful venture when in reality it is a green light that their pursuit is worth fighting for.

It takes courage and faith to accept one's shortcomings and failings to the loving father who issued an open invitation to come to His gracious throne to exchange weakness for strength. It is amazing how much a difference the grace of God makes in putting us over our deficiencies and character flaws. No matter at what point we are up the ladder the need for grace and mercy that God gives to the believing enquirer can never be overestimated.

The bible on Habits

Habits can be learned

Proverbs 22:6

Train up a child in the way he should go and when he is old he would not depart from it.

Habits can be conquered

Philippians 2:13

I can do all things through Christ who gives me strength.

Habits determine life's outcome

Galatians 6:9

And let us not be weary in well doing for we shall reap if we faint not.

Daily habits determine greatness

Joshua 1:8

This book of the law shall not depart out of your mouth but you shall meditate on it day and night that you may observe to do all that is written therein, then shall you make your way prosperous and you would have good success.

Both scripture and science agree that there is an association between repetition and habit formation and that daily habits are potent indicators of future success.

Chapter Two Summary

1. The secret to success is hidden in daily seeds of habits sown into the garden of life. Success and failures are never sudden events.

2. If you don't like the fruit you are reaping check the seed you are sowing.

3. Habits are acquired patterns of behaviour that have become almost automatic as a result of frequent repetition.

4. Psychologists believe habits are formed when a reaction (response) is linked to an event (stimulus) for long enough.

5. The unique physical and chemical structure of the brain makes it relatively difficult to break old habits and form new ones. However ones formed these same features, promote preservation of new habits.

6. Negative habits that are contrary to success can be subtle and insidious. The first step to correcting them lies in awareness

7. Negative habits can be identified by asking for divine revelation, asking the opinion of trusted family and friends and enlisting help of relevant experts.

8. Observation of patterns in areas of failure acceptance of identified habits without excuses and developing an action plan to correct them are additional crucial steps to ridding unhelpful habits.

9. It is crucial to be **realistic, committed, consistent** and **courageous** in an attempt to cultivate pro success habits.

10. The bible teaches that habits can be learnt and conquered. It also teaches that habits determine life's outcome and daily habits determine success.

Chapter Reflective & Action points

1. Write down steps you would take this week to identify anti success habits in one aspect of your life.

2. List the anti success habits you have identified in that aspect of your life

3. Identify the most crucial and pertinent habit that needs to change

4. Devise a clear written plan to address and change this habit.

The starting point of all achievement is desire.

Napoleon Hill.
(Author of Think & Grow Rich)

The decisive test of desire is the price the bearer is prepared to pay in exchange for its accomplishment.

T. Ayodele Ajayi

CHAPTER 3

Desire Habits of Giants

The journey to significance always begins with a desire. I am yet to see any human who has made their mark in any sphere of life without a preceding burning desire to be an achiever. Such desire and corresponding action is a hallmark of Olympic medallists, company directors, and successful entrepreneurs. "I woke up and found I had become great" are story lines only for fairy tale novels. They never occupy in reality.

An interesting and revealing Granada Television documentary film *The Up Series* commenced in 1964 and augmented every seven years thereafter, suggested that one of the most telling indicators of a child's future is the interests and preferences they express around age seven. The insights from this land –breaking cohort study of fourteen British seven year olds, encourage adults to revisit their childhood to recapture what their desires and interests were as it is believed to hold a clue to their future. I was initially dismissive of the report as I did not find it true in my experience. However, on a more introspective search I could remember my desire to study Medicine dates back to as far back as I can remember of my childhood. Furthermore, I found that my desire to research, collate and present information predates my college days. Over the years, my natural endowment in the use of written language has always been subtly evident. It is no wonder several years later I am taking on the challenge of writing an inspirational book.

Giants take their desires seriously enough to dare to take action to aid their manifestation. What is your desire? Do you desire to see discipline and order returned to local schools? Does your heart yearn with desire to see credible and accountable governance of your nation's resources? Or yours is a longing to help pregnant teenagers fulfil their potentials despite their initial setbacks. The desire to build adequately resourced orphanages to offer a loving nurturing start to abandoned children or orphans can become a reality. Whatever your intense desire is, take it seriously, because it could hold the crucial clue to an area you are destined to succeed.

Your desire is usually a predictor of those you have been sent to serve. Giants are perceptive enough to respond to the natural inclinations and desires to help others. They have learnt to listen to the rhythm of their hearts as it is drawn to the cry of those to whom they are called.

Here are a few truth be in mind on the relationship of desire to greatness.

Desire is a God given ability

Every human was born with a desire to succeed and excel. It is a divinely endowed inherent craving. Who teaches the toddler to "want to do it myself"? Desire is given to pull us towards a yet unrealised but noble future. It is therefore never to be ignored.

The question one may ask is what ever happened to the desire of those humans who appear to lack them. Negative life experiences, initial set backs and cynical responses to these desires have sometimes driven them into the recesses of human hearts. The critical impact of a belittling parent, the "who-do –you-think- you –are" stares and caustic comments from peers and superiors have nailed the coffin of many childhood dreams and aspirations which may well have been fulfilled by pursuit. The truth however is, if you dug well enough you can unearth those treasures buried in the rumble of your unsavoury past.

Desire is starting point of greatness

Desire always precedes outstanding success in any endeavour. Success is a medal reserved for those who desire it intensely enough to go all out in its pursuit. Satiety is a function of hunger. Do you have a desire for exceptional success in your career, marriage or ministry or are you happy to settle for the average? There is no pride or shame in wishing to go all the way.

Desire births passion to overcome obstacles

Desire, when it lingers enough and is allowed to thrive by much rumination always gives birth to passion for actualisation. It is this passion that drives and motivates to overcome apparently insurmountable obstacles in the success journey. No human tells the truth that says his or her journey to greatness was a straight unhindered course. Through the passion born out of intense desire such feats, such as charting the course of the Atlantic and travelling to the moon have been achieved.

Desire births resolute decisions

The truth is at the bottom line there is no human who really does not desire to be a success in any of life's endeavours. The sad bit however, is that very few convert that desire for success into a resolute decision to become an achiever.

The irrevocable decision to pursue a desire until it culminates in success backed up by corresponding action is what differentiates achievers from daydreamers. Pursuit is the decisive test of desire.

How much do you long to succeed in your business or ministry? What price are you willing to pay to ensure your marriage is a success and your children turn out well? Every giant is a person who has counted the cost of success and decided to pay it anyway.

What the bible says about desires

Desire for success and achievement is from God

Philippians 2:13

It is God who worketh in you both to will and to do of his good pleasure.

Contrary to what some unknowing- people believe, the desire for excellence and success is a God given one. It is not evil to desire success in marriage, business, career or ministry. Christianity and excellence are mutually inclusive rather than exclusive. And excellence invariably attracts success. In fact, all good and perfect gifts are from God (James 1:17) and He would not give them out if He does not expect us to desire them. A careful review of the creation story in the first chapters of genesis should convince doubters that God is the author of desires for excellence. At the end of creation He declared all things He created were good.

God can and would beat any desire for success made of him

Ephesians 3:20

God has the ability to make anyone succeed above their wildest dreams or imagination. He would match and beat any desire made of Him as long as His principles are upheld and followed.

God's own desire is all round Humans success

3John2

Beloved, I wish above all things that thou prosper and be in health, even as thy soul prospereth.

It is not God's desire for his children to succeed in their business but have a failed marriage or ministry. Neither is it His will to succeed in ministry but have wayward children or be impoverished.

Chapter Three Summary

1. Success always begins with a desire.

2. Research shows that the childhood desires and interests are a reflection of potential areas of excellence.

3. Successful people take their desires seriously and take action to achieve them.

4. Desire is a divine endowment given to all humans to pull us towards a noble future.

5. Negative life experiences and hostile environment sometimes buries these desires and conceals them.

6. A thorough heart searching can unearth these buried desires.

7. Desire when allowed to thrive by rumination births passion that motivates to overcome obstacles to fulfilment.

8. The path to success is laden with hurdles and obstacles but they can be overcome.

9. Desire when it births a resolution backed up by action is what separates achievers from daydreamers.

10. The bible teaches that

    a.   Desires to succeed are from God

    c.   God would beat any desire for success made of Him

    b.   God desires all round success for His children.

Nothing just happens, somebody, somewhere picked up the price tag and paid it.

-Dr Albert Odulele, Pastor Glory House International Churches

The longer I live, the more I am certain that the great difference between the feeble and the powerful, between the great and the insignificant, is energy-invincible determination- a purpose once fixed, and then death or victory.

-Sir Thomas Fowell Buxton (Nineteenth Century English Abolitionist and Social Reformer)

Quality is never an accident; it is always the result of high intention, sincere effort, intelligent direction and skilful execution. It represents wise choice of many alternatives.

-Anon.

CHAPTER 4

Decision Habits of Giants

The irrevocable decision to pursue a desire until it culminates in success backed up by corresponding action is what differentiates achievers from daydreamers.

A careful study of achievers shows that a desire not backed by a personal decision to succeed achieves little. Most achievers can recount sometimes to the date and time when they made the irresolute decision not to relent until their desire becomes a reality. The desire for success must go beyond a wishful thought, which is translated into a promise to self to do all that is ethically required to achieve. Is your desire backed up by a firm decision to pay the price of diligence to see your hearts desire?

It is interesting that many achievers were spurred on to success by what may have been perceived as adversity or setbacks. There are ample examples in history to prove that adverse life experiences can either be used as an excuse for failure or the motivation for success.

I was intrigued to read Oprah Winfrey, America's leading Talk Show host's biography. Listed *by* Forbes' international rich list as the world's only black billionaire in 2004, 2005, and 2006 and as the first black woman billionaire in world history; Winfrey was the product of a casual intimate encounter between her unmarried teenage parents. Oprah's mother Vernita was a house cleaner and her father was a coal miner who later became a barber. She started her early life raised by her grandmother who was so poor Oprah often had to wear clothes made from potato sacks. Poor as they were her grandmother handed to her a Godly heritage by taking her to church and teaching her to read by age three.

In subsequent years, Winfrey quickly suffered the adversity of being sexually molested by cousins, uncles and a family friend starting from the age of nine. She had become a teenage mother by fourteen and suffered the additional tragedy of losing her infant son. Yet only three years later she had won Miss Tennessee beauty pageant and began her media career. Her career revealed the gem covered in dross of initial adversity and humble beginnings. It is no wonder she is quoted as saying "it doesn't matter who you are, where you come from, the ability to triumph begins with you. Always!

The ability to triumph always begins with the person who defies current or past adversity and converts them to the motivation for success rather excuse for failure. I am inclined to believe that the more successful a person is the less likely there are to make excuses. Many potential Media gurus, singing icons, film stars, Nobel laurels, successful entrepreneurs and great ministers of the gospel ended up as nobody because of one excuse or the other.

If we let them hold us down there will always be enough legitimate excuses for failing to achieve our maximum potential. Somebody has said that one of the greatest deterrents to success is a condition called *excusitis*, an inflammation of the excuse making glands. How many times have you heard people blame underachievement on lack of opportunities, poor parenting, difficult background or discrimination? At other times, the *excusitis* is the reason we give for not pursuing our dreams now. "I am too busy with other endeavours", I hear the words echo. I would wait until the time and conditions are right and optimal.

I have however realised in my study and personal experience that the time and condition would never be optimal until one makes now the right and optimal one by a firm decision of commitment. There would never be an optimal time to return to college or start that postgraduate degree you have been putting off for a few years. You will never feel you have sufficient spare time to learn to play the saxophone or speak French or German.

My heart bleeds each time I hear another unfamiliar yet peculiar story of the young immigrant who left their home county in search of the Golden Fleece. They leave the support and comfort of familiar social milieu with a view of improving their lot by obtaining further or higher education in the western world. On arrival they are waylaid by their predecessor's how- difficult- it- is to -make –ends- meet- here stories. They start off taking on a menial job to "make ends meet" and save up to go to pay their tuition. But alas, the hopes of financial independence of these young, brilliant and gifted potential achievers turns to despair as the weeks turns to months and the months to years but the optimal time and condition to pursue their dreams remain elusive. Most of them end up frustrated and despondent trapped in jobs below their potential without resources to pursue their dreams of further education.

If what you have just read tells your story, I encourage you that your decision today could be your first step up the rung of the social ladder. The story can change if you would purpose in your heart that despite the hardship and lack of resources you would pursue your dreams. A way always shows up for the one who has an irresolute will.

Waiting for Aunt Martha?

I am reminded of a true -life story I once heard which emphasises the import of deciding now where you want to be and immediately taking steps to achieve your dreams despite negating circumstances. This story told by Brian Tracey, one of the world's leading experts on time management and personal and organisational success is worth repeating.

Mr Tracey was the Keynote speaker at a leading organisation's business dinner where he had the privilege of being seated next to a well turned out, confident and friendly couple who told him about their journey to financial independence.

The man had been a fire fighter and his wife had stayed home to raise their two children. They were the average American working class family living in a two bedroom small house. This man made "just enough" to keep the family going and they had no real concerns because as soon as Aunt Martha died they would be rich. Aunt Martha was an apparently wealthy relative who had confided in them that she would bequeath them when she passes away.

The couple narrated how they grew from their twenty's to their thirties and Aunt Martha rather than show evidence of waning appeared to be growing stronger. Over this period, the family continued to treat Aunt

Martha well. The children sent cards and she was a regular dinner guest. Eventually the couple's breakthrough moment came when one day the lady asked her husband over the kitchen table- "How about if Aunt Martha lived another twenty years?". After all, there is longevity in the family. Are we going to continue to wait here twiddling our fingers and waiting for her to pass away?

The husband, at this point agreed with his wife, it was time to act and began exploring business opportunities. He eventually took up an additional job in the evenings and saved enough to buy their first business franchise. As a result of commitment and hard work the business fared well enough for him to resign his fire fighter position and concentrate full time on building the family's chain of franchises, which turned out with phenomenal success. I can imagine you are as keen as Mr Tracey was in knowing how the story ended.

True to prediction, Aunt Martha lived another twenty years. When she eventually died all the nephews and nieces from both sides of her family were gathered in anticipation of being bequeathed as well. There was however two surprises for this expectant waiting crowd at the reading of her will. Apparently, like the couple in our story, Aunt Martha had promised everyone else they were her favourites and would be beneficiaries to her wealth when she eventually passed away. The other shocker came when the will was read. Aunt Martha to everyone's dismay had been penniless for many years, living off the good graces of family members who were waiting in anticipation of becoming wealthy when she passed away.

What Aunt Martha are you waiting to die before you make a crucial decision about your future and back it up with corresponding action? The time would never be right to start the money saving habit. Personal finance experts have rightly said that the ideal is to save ten percent of ones annual income. They have however also warned that it is easier to spend what you have left over after you have saved, than save what you have left over after you have spent. In other words, savings should be treated as an essential expenditure on a personal budget plan.

Until you make it by your own decision and action, the time to start spending quality time with your family will never arrive. There would not be the optimal time to start investing in community service, giving money to charities or paying your tithes. The time to take on that additional managerial responsibility you are being offered will never come until you face the situation and take up the offer anyway. Do not relegate yourself to the league of the *would –have- been* who are still waiting, albeit now with regret and bitterness at what could have been but never was because rather than seize the moment they were waiting for the proverbial optimal time that only belongs to the never land.

It has been said that the more successful people are the less likely they are to make excuses.

Opportunities

The other commonly cited excuse for not making a decision now is the perception of paucity of opportunities. Many talented people blame their indecision and underachievement on lack of opportunities. The colour, accent, and background are quoted as excuses when some successful people of similar circumstances have cited the same for their success. The truth is opportunity abounds all around for the one who has decided to find them irrespective of their past and current circumstances.

It is fascinating and encouraging to know that about fifty percent of Chief Executive Officers of the Fortune 500 companies had a C or C- average in college. Even more interesting is the fact that about seventy- five percent of all American Presidents were in the bottom half of their class. The subtle message in this intriguing statistics is that where one is now does not matter as much as where one decides one wants to be tomorrow as long as the decision is matched by corresponding consistent action in the desired direction.

Fear of mistakes

The lack of decision and positive action is at other times a consequence of the fear of making mistakes. Achievers are those who spurred on by the decision to succeed defy the crippling thought of making errors. Teddy Roosevelt said he who makes no mistakes makes no progress. There are not too many in the winner's league that made their hit at the first attempt. Statistics have it that the average America Millionaire had been or nearly bankrupt for three times before achieving their dream of financial independence.

I agree with the one who said, *I would rather try and fail than never try and never know I could succeed.*

Rev Timothy Kolade said a beautician can help you make up your face, but only you can make up your mind. Each human has been endowed with the ability and privilege to decide. I have come to learn that any one who will achieve has to make that personal decision to do so. There are no indecisive people are the top.

Dr Myles Munroe defined mediocrity as a region bothered on the north by compromise, on the south by indecision, on the east by past thinking and on the west by lack of vision. He cautioned that prolonged indecisiveness is a vision killer, which drains the joy of life. Life losses it's zest and fervour when decisions are not made at opportune times to capture the moment.

Diminishing Intent

The next pressing reason why each would- be achiever must never delay decision to act is the operation of the law of diminishing intent. The law states that the longer you wait to do something you know you should do now the greater the chances you will never actually do it. It only takes asking one who has passed the prime of their life without much to show for the years to prove this law. The stories of books which were conceived, but never written or published are countless. The undeveloped research themes, the abandoned PhD thesis and business plans, the unanswered ministry call and waylaid careers all testify to the credence of the law of diminishing intent. Take the bulls by the horns and act now rather than wait for the optimal time that never comes.

The fear of criticism and becoming unpopular is another common factor that causes delay in decision to pursue conviction of purpose. Achievers the world over are those who have counted the cost of following their dreams, turned their face to their goals and their backs to jeerers. David Schwartz in his book *The Magic of thinking Big* noted no one does anything worthwhile for which he is not criticised. Dare to take a survey of anyone whose life counts for much around you and you would find out that each one, without exception has learnt to use the dirty comments of critics to manure their path to achievement.

Hope is not lost. Every achiever or winner you see today is an ex loser who got fed up of defeat, dared to find the secret of winning and persevered in practicing what they discovered until their results changed their terrain. The relevant question to ask ones self at this point is whether one is indeed fed up with the status quo. If the answer is in the affirmative, is the discontent intense enough to pursue change? How tenacious is your decision not to relent until alternative outcome is achieved?

Goals

Today could be the day you decide to ditch the losers club. The secret of getting ahead is getting started (Mark Twain). Achievers get started by setting themselves SMART goals. The truth is no one ever stumbles into success without a goal. Goals are invariably the evidence of a decision to change the future.

Statistics suggest that only three percent of adults have clear written goals. Yet those few accomplish five to ten times as much as people of equal or better education and ability but who for whatever reason , have never taken the time to write out exactly what is it they want.(Brian Tracy 2004). Another statistic says that an additional ten percent of adults have goals, which are not committed to writing. They keep them in their heads. The three percent with written goals and plans accomplish fifty to hundred times more during their lifetime than the ten percent with unwritten goals. These figures leaves one wondering how dismal the fate must be, of the rest eighty-seven percent who neither have goals nor write them down.

Goals are essential to success as air is to life. I read with interest the outcome of a recent Department for Children, Schools and Families study, among school leavers linking low aspiration with underperformance in the GCSE examinations. Young white males from poor backgrounds relative to all other ethnic groups are less likely to achieve the minimum five expected A to C grade ranges in the examinations. Poor expectation imposed by the nurturing environment has been cited as the main reason for the underachievement of these lads.

Goals are crucial to success for several reasons. For starters, they represent a mental picture and internal blueprint of where a person is headed. In consequence, goals inevitably shape and direct the future. My heart sinks each time I listen to the pitiful story of another youngster who is approaching their A level examinations or in final year of undergraduate studies without any inkling of what they would like to achieve thereafter. One without goals is like a ship at sea without a rudder. Such ship is at the mercy of every wind that blows and the chances of reaching a desired destination safely is very grim. Achievers are those who use the tool of goal setting to carve out their desired future.

Goals also assist the visionary in recognising and harnessing current opportunities. Many opportunities for achievement and advancement are lost due to lack of discernment. The sheer process of goal setting stimulates a quest for opportunities and avenues to achieve them. Successful people are those whose goals and its pursuit alert them to opportunities that go unnoticed or despised by the non- achievers.

Goal setting appears to have an impetus in itself for achievement. It attracts the resources for achievement. Have you observed how those who set goals and are determined to achieve them always seem to eventually find the financial, time and human resources for achievement? Could it be that the simple process of setting goals creates an atmosphere of faith and possibilities in the subconscious, which translates to the physical and culminates in realisation?

Growth in any endeavour is invariably the result of goals. It is never a natural thoughtless process. Even the thought of a neonate growing naturally into an infant, a toddler and eventually a well -rounded adult suggests it is not without the conscious effort of the nurturer. One could imagine what the outcome would be if the new born was abandoned at birth without anyone taking responsibility for supplying basic physical and emotional needs. Achievers are those who recognise goals set a lid on progress and utilise goal setting to their advantage.

It is rarely the case that much growth is made in any organisation without an effort. Churches, businesses, families and corporate organisations are all subject to this assertion albeit to varying dimensions.

The association of goals setting to success is also reflected in its influence on choices. Goal setters are people who make choices based on their desired outcome rather than current circumstances. I was intrigued to learn how for many years President Barak Obama had carefully kept to the straight and narrow path of life in view of his aspiration for American presidency. Achievers like Obama many times opt for the austere relative to the flamboyant in consciousness of the day the record books would be opened. How many politicians or those of high social status have suffered a sudden decline due to indiscreet acts committed many years before they came into the public glare. Those who have their eyes on high places in their field must also learn to keep their appetites in check. Allow your goals to influence your choices as one careless act could jeopardise a carefully planned future.

Goals also aid success by hastening their own accomplishment. The human brain functions better and more readily cooperates to deliver a written goal than with a nebulous aspiration that is carried in the mind. Written goals as previously mentioned also increase up to ten folds the odds of achievement.

Life would be a drudgery of routines without habitually setting and meeting goals. The quest for achievement, which results in goal setting and subsequent achievement makes life exciting and worthwhile. No wonder statistics suggest that those who retire and keep their mind and body occupied with worthwhile activities tend to live longer than contemporaries who put up their feet after retirement.

There is something about written goals that holds one accountable to self and important others and keeps one on track whatever the climate. Let me share my own experience of a protracted postgraduate training and how, without the aid of a goal I had set myself before ever going into medical school I would have abandoned my psychiatry training. My initial thoughts to concentrate on qualifying before starting a family did not go to plan and as the family grew, it became more challenging to dedicate time to studying. I recount clearly how after each season of examination failure I reminded myself how giving up was not an option. After five attempts at my final examination I achieved my goal with a even firmer conviction that goal setting is crucial to success.

Are you a goal setter or you are just living your life driven by the winds? Goals are an evidence of a decision to be an achiever. Management experts use the acronym SMART to define goals.

Specific- The human brain relates better to specific clearly defined goals. The specification starts with putting pen on paper. It is not enough to want to be a better Pastor or a more efficient treasurer?

Measurable- Goals must be measurable in terms of monetary value, standards, numbers or quality. *I want my business to grow bigger by next year*! Is this in terms of doubling your turn over or tripling your workforce?

Achievable-Goals must be achievable, challenging enough to stretch ones ability and dependence on the omnipotent but also within boundaries of what ones faith can take on.

Realistic- These are goals that take into consideration the available resources whilst factoring in divine help and providence

Time Limited-Goals must be bounded by time as this helps one to measure performance. There should not be any term paper, school project or thesis embarked on without a time line. Time line entails more than just setting the final deadline, it includes setting deadlines for each of the deliverables factoring in unanticipated delays and detours. A practical time period demarcation is to set short, medium and long term goals. The time period for each of these goals are one, three and ten years respectively.

The future begins now. It is suffice to conclude this chapter with this final admonition, quoting from Johann Wolfgan Von Goethe. *Whatever you do, or dream you can, begin it. Boldness has genius, power and magic in it.*

The bible on Decisions and Goals

There is an opportune time for decisions

Ecclesiastes 3:1

To everything there is a season and a time for every purpose under heaven.

There is an opportune time to face the situation, make a decision to be who you were born to be and stand by that decision. Now is that time for anyone who finds themselves reading these words today.

People shape the future by choices (Decisions)

God has granted to all humans the power of choice to decide what the outcome of the future would be like whether brilliant or otherwise. Joshua24:15 illustrates how powerfully endowed humans are with decision to change the future.

God always backs and support resolute decision makers

God always supports everyone who dares to make and stand by their right decisions. He provided Abraham with a ram as an alternative sacrifice for his son Isaac after Abraham decided to obey God's command at all cost (Genesis 22). He granted Esther overwhelming favour before her husband king Ahasuerus resulting in the rescue of her people from Haman's genocide plot

(Esther 4:16,17, 8:3-16). It was the same God who backed up Nehemiah's decision to rebuild the broken walls of Jerusalem (Nehemiah 2:5), gave him favour before King Artaxerxes (Nehemiah 2:6-8) and granted him faithful supporters to complete the project successfully (Nehemiah 7:1-3). How about the divine enabling ministry of an angel that Jesus the Messiah received as he struggled in Gethsemane with His decision to die on the cross to redeem the human race? (Luke 22:43)

Be assured that the same divine grace available for men of old still awaits the person who resolves to follow their God given dreams.

God frowns at back sliding

Luke 9:62

No one who puts his hands to the plough and looks back is worthy of the kingdom of God.

Giants are ex-weaklings who decided to grow in strength and despite all odds kept at the work until their results became apparent. No one who starts on a course but turns back, ever win the trophy.

Excuses abort purposes

Ecclesiastes 11:4

He who observes the wind would not sow and he who regards the clouds would not reap

There would always be enough apparently genuine excuses not to initiate or continue to pursue one's dreams.

Visions should be written

Habakkuk 2:2-3

And the Lord answered me, and said, write the Vision, and make it plain upon tables, that he may run that readeth it. For the vision is yet for an appointed time, but at the end it would speak and not lie: though it tarry, wait for it; because it would surely come, it will not tarry.

Chapter Four Summary

1. Desire for success without a corresponding decision and action achieves little.

2. Many achievers in history used their setbacks as a motivation for success rather than an excuse for failure.

3. The ability to triumph always begins with a personal choice to triumph.

4. There would always be apparently legitimate excuses for failing to pursue one's dreams.

5. The optimal time to pursue a dream would never automatically present itself until one by personal decision and commitment convert the now into the optimal.

6. There are many opportunities to excel for the one who rather than cite current circumstances as excuse, convert them into motivation to excel.

7. Given statistics of Chief Executive Officers and American Presidents, poor educational achievement in high school is not sufficient reason not to achieve one's full adult potential. Your decision to change your current status

and the corresponding actions backing it is more important than your current status.

8. Achievers are those who overcome their fear of making errors and step out to fulfil their dreams any way. There are few achievers without an experience of apparent failure in their track to success.

9. Decision to excel is always a personal responsibility.

10. Life losses it's zest and fervour when opportune moments to make decisions are missed.

11. The longer execution of a right decision is delayed the greater the chances of complete abortion.

12. Achievers are those who despite criticism of others pursue and achieve. It is rare to achieve anything of worth without being criticised.

13. All winners are ex losers who found and practised the secret of winning until they obtained results.

14. Success is rarely a chance event. Goals are invariably the evidence of a decision for a different future.

15. Written goals increases the chances of their achievement by up to 10 folds.

16. Goals inevitably shape and direct the future. Achievers use this knowledge to their advantage.

17. Goals help in recognition and harnessing prevailing opportunities.

18. Life is unexciting and boring without a life style of setting and meeting goals.

19. Goals apparently carry a self -fulfilling force by attracting relevant resources.

20. Growth in any organisation is invariably the result of goal setting.

21. Goals influence choices thereby promoting growth.

22. Goals must be **SMART-Specific, Measurable, Achievable, Realistic and Time bounded.**

23. The scriptures teach that
    Humans shape the future by personal choices
    God always supports irresolute decision makers
    God frowns at backsliding
    Excuses abort great purposes

Action plan & reflection

1. Identify one area of your life in which you are waiting for the optimal timing to take positive action.

2. Is this waiting justifiable in the light of what you have just read? What excuses have you been giving for waiting?

3. Write down a SMART goal on this area of life

4. List a systematic action plan to move from inactivity to positive action in this area?

"Personal development is your springboard to personal excellence. Ongoing, continuous, non-stop personal development literally assures you that there is no limit to what you can accomplish."

**Brian Tracy, International Sales &
Time management guru**

"No one limits your growth but you. If you want to earn more, learn more. That means you'll work harder for a while; that means you'll work longer for a while. But you'll be paid for your extra effort with enhanced earnings down the road."

Tom Hopkins

CHAPTER 5

Development habit of Giants

Everyone was born with all the potentials of becoming a giant but whether they eventually become one is a matter of choice and effort. In addition to having a desire, which is translated into a dream, all achievers go the extra mile of taking progressive relevant steps towards realisation.

In reality like precious metals, which are mined in raw and impure ores and require intense chemical and heat treatment for purification, humans require recognition, refining and utilisation of naturally endowed resources to become achievers and giants. It is the failure to recognise, develop or utilise these talents or natural endowments that result in falling short of maximizing potential.

Most of us do not have a problem with recognising our talents but development without which optimal utilisation cannot occur is sometimes a challenge. Allow me to share with you the reasons why development of talents, skills and abilities is so pivotal to achievement of success.

Development optimises benefits of abilities

Like gold, silver and all other precious metals, the beauty and value of natural and acquired abilities can only be fully appreciated in their purest refined forms. The process of refining however takes time and diligent and consistent application of appropriate effort. That baritone voice would be of little use to the orchestra until it is cultured through seasons of training. Your grace of hospitality and care of others may not command attention in the high places of society until it is recognised and refined by completing a relevant diploma or degree programme. The natural knack to motivate and mentor others to fulfil their purpose would command more personal & monetary reward when refined by a personal performance coaching training.

Development eliminates regression

The next case for self- development in order to be an achiever is in Pat Riley a basketball coach's words-*if you are not getting better you are getting worse.* Indeed, there is no stagnancy in life. A man may delude himself with the thought that he is stationary but not regressing but the reality is he is regressing who is not progressing whilst his comrades are. It may only take a while before the reality dawns. Achievers the world over recognise the need to keep updating their skills, acquiring fresh ones and taking on fresh challenges.

The world is in an ever -evolving phase of astronomical growth and development. A failure to consistently update talents and skills by development would result in a handicap in meeting the challenges and demands of the contemporary world. Only three decades ago, the now commonplace international trading and globalization which the internet age has allowed, would have been inconceivable. Yet in the 21st century world, no one can make a lasting impact in any field of endeavour without an appreciable level of computer dexterity and skill.

The stakes of expectation are rising by the minute with globalisation. The requirement to be multi skilled, multi lingual and multi tasking is becoming standard expectation in the market place. A careful observation of the trends in Europe reveals how much emphasis our European cousins place on their children being fluent readers and writers of the English Language. There is however, a concern that such enthusiasm does not appear to be reciprocated among English youngsters towards learning major European languages. It is difficult not to imagine the unilingual English being at a disadvantage to multilingual European cousins as Europe becomes more unified.

Development sets a lid on achievement

Personal development is necessary for potential and established achievers because leaders in any field or endeavour are the lids over their organisations. A company cannot excel above the vision forecasted by its board of directors. The team leader sets the standard for his subordinates. A congregant rarely grows spiritually to excel above his presiding pastor. The head of a family unit sets a lid over the economic and spiritual welfare of his under aged children. Leaders must therefore place very high demands and standards of achievement on themselves in recognition that they dictate the pace for the led.

The simple truth of leaders being lids explains why some committed and talented employees sometimes leave organisations. It unravels the puzzle of spiritual, devoted church members moving on to another church when they realize the presiding pastor does not have the spiritual influence and soundness to take them to the place of their dreams.

Development results in excellence, which attracts reward

Excellence always results from consistent effort of self-development. In truth the top rungs of the ladders in business, ministry, music, art and various professions are reserved for those who would stretch and develop themselves to meet the high standards of spiritual, moral, technical and inter personal competencies required of such offices. The remuneration in money and status is a function of the value that one brings to the market place. Value is a function of excellence.

According to Jim Rohn ,success is what one attracts by becoming an attractive person. In order to be an achiever the challenge is to work harder on oneself than on ones job. Rohn, an internationally renowned business entrepreneur and public speaker learnt from his mentor Rod Schoaff that the man who works hard on his job makes a living but the one who works hard on himself makes a fortune. Indeed no one according to John Maxwell can do the minimum and expect to reach his maximum potential.

One cannot agree more with the one who said "If a man writes a better book, preaches a better sermon, or makes a better mouse trap than his neighbour; even if he builds his house in the woods the world will make a beaten path to his door". The world's system in all it's spheres still pays credit to excellence.

Self-development may take several forms. It could entail formal or self -education, training, coaching, tutelage and or mentoring.

Allow me to share with you a few self -development habits of giants.

Personal choice

A personal choice backed with corresponding action in self -development is a hallmark of giants. And there is no negotiation about this truth.

Ralph J Cordiner, former Chairman of the Board of the General Electric Company once described the personal choice crucial to self development in this manner- "We need from every man who aspires to leadership-for himself and for his company- a determination to undertake a personal program of self-development. Nobody is going to order a man to develop..........Whether a man lags behind or moves ahead in his specialty is a matter of his own personal application. This is something which takes time, work and sacrifice."

Needs assessment

Giants assess and recognise their development needs and set themselves goals formulated into a plan to meet those needs. A needs assessment could be conducted informally or in a formal fashion using validated tools. Have you identified what training, education or additional skills you need to fulfil your short, medium and long- term goals?

Identify relevant resources

Giants are people who not only identify their needs for development but also find the best and most suitable resource to meet those needs. These days there is a preponderance of resource both on and off line that it is ridiculously inexcusable to cite paucity as a reason for development failure. For the keen searcher there is enough resource out there to fit every financial and time budget.

The library abounds with books, the internet with information and the colleges with courses. The question to ask oneself is whether posterity would accept the excuse that currently holds one from self- development and achievement. Giants are those who find a way round their excuses to develop themselves. Indeed according to the Chinese proverb "when the student is ready the teacher cannot but show up!

The decisive test advocated by David Schwartz in his *Magic of thinking Big* is a sure but simple test to apply to self -development resources. According to him, any training must provide three things- content (What to do); method (how to do it) and thirdly produce results.

Transform information into action

Mortimer Adler, author of *How to read a book* once said-"In the case of good books, the point is not to see how many of them you can get through, but how many can get through to you". Knowledge acquired from personal development is of no use if it is not translated into consistent action that results in progressive habits culminating in achievement. Giants recognise this truth and use it to their advantage. I write with a passion and prayer that this book would not become a mere number on the read list, but it's reading would result in purposeful action placing the reader in the roll call of giants who leave footprints on the sand of time.

Allow me to share a few self -development lessons from the life of giants

Daily life long learning

Giants in all fields and specialties have a self- style of daily life long learning. They live each day being alert to lessons and gleaning as much from their experiences as possible. No matter at what level they are they are never too learned, skilled or experienced to ask questions. They recognise like Ray Kroc that "as long as you are green you are growing. As soon as you're ripe you start to rut".

The life long learning of giants is manifested in

1. *Purposeful planned learning.* You cannot become a giant at what you do except you make regular learning a planned, purposeful and prioritised activity. Achievers never leave their learning to chance or casual encounters.

2. *Learning something new each day*. Whether it is a new vocabulary, verse of scripture, or a new skill, or management tip giants ensure learning is a daily experience. In the palm top dot. com age, carrying around a bible, dictionary or thesaurus is no longer a cumbersome experience. With some careful consideration, every one can make daily learning a life style.

3. *Reading each day*. Most leaders in their field are avid readers. Readers are simply leaders. You cannot stay ahead of the pack in your game without keeping abreast with daily developments. In addition to a dedicated period of studying the bible each day, it is expedient to have a plan in place to ensure daily relevant study.

Let me share with you any interesting statistic that drives home the importance of reading in achieving success.

The average Chief Executive Officer (CEO)in America reads four to five books in a month while the average American reads one book per year. Sixty percent of those who read one book don't even get past the first chapter in that one book. The average CEO of a fortune 500 company will earn 536 times the salary of the average employee of the company he runs.

This means the employee of the company he runs will work for a year and a half to equal the salary of the CEO for one day.

Their reading habit is not the only difference in their lifestyles but it is one of the major differences. (Ron white Jim Rohn ezine April 30 2008)

4. In addition to maintaining healthy reading habits, giants have a structured method of recording and retrieving the knowledge acquired. What benefit is gained if when acquired knowledge is needed it is not readily available. If you must become a giant devise a personal structured, easily retrievable method of storing knowledge and experiences.

The use of highlighters or markers to identify remarkable text is desirable. An even better practice is to use a colour -coded scheme to distinguish text requiring action, giving instruction, or referring to a quote. Others adopt the method of summarising chapters in bullet points for future reference. Whatever method is adopted must be such that allows knowledge to be easily stored and retrieved when required for action or reference.

5. Regularly keeping and updating a list of helpful literature and books you intend to read in the future is a desirable achieving habit to cultivate. My personal method of ensuring I keep a record of books that I plan to read in future is to keep a viable regularly updated wish list on my amazon.com account.

6. Another practice that enhances a daily reading habit is maintaining subscriptions to relevant e magazines (ezines).Several international personal development agencies send out periodical free emails featuring various relevant articles by internationally renowned names in their field of expertise.

7. *Life style of teaching others* .The old maxim of learning-"See one, do one and teach one" remains true as ever. A habit of, not only acquiring but impacting knowledge practised by giants further enhances their personal development .If you wish to be better at your trade or endeavour imitate the giants and start teaching others what you already know.

8. *Growing from mistakes.* Giants are those who not only learn from positive but also negative experiences. There are two methods of learning. You could learn either by direct observation of how to do things right or by recognition of

how not to do it the next time round .Mistakes only become fatal when nothing is learnt from them.

Air travel today has become a very popular and relatively safe and trusted means of transport. It was not always so however, but for the learning culture of the aviation industry which ensures every air disaster or near miss is transformed into a learning experience.

9. *Self- scrutiny.* Leaders are those who avail themselves of the benefit of daily self- scrutiny. They constantly develop by asking the opinion of peers, superiors and subordinates in refining their productivity. The 360 degrees feedback process is now embraced by several professional groups as a means of constructive self -evaluation. Giants need to be secure enough to invite others to constructive cast an eye on and offer feedback on the quality of their work.

10. *Self -exposure.* Giants are not ashamed to leave their own domains and territories to explore and learn from peers. They do not deem it a sign of ignorance to ask others what works for them

11. *Change embracing.* If you wish to climb up the ladder in your field, you must be open to change. The giants in the society are those who do not lose sleep about relinquishing the old for the new and better methods of conducting their affairs. The one who refuses change when it is mandatory will sooner than later find they have become a tombstone, a mere landmark of success that once was.

12. *Self- investment.* It is rarely the case that one would be able to learn much without making money, time and sometimes relationship investment. I firmly agree with Benjamin Franklin that "if we take the pennies from our pockets and put them in our heads, our heads will then fill up our pockets once again". My dear wife knows how much easier it is for me to walk away from a suit shop without a purchase than from a bookshop without a book.

What the bible says about personal development

1. Jesus' parable of the talents in Matthew 25:14-33

Teaches every human is divinely endowed with talents. These talents are meant to be developed with a view to profiting. Those who fail to develop their talents fall short of divine expectation.

2. Timothy 2:15

Study to show yourself approved unto God, a workman that does not need to be ashamed rightly dividing the word of truth.

In this admonition of Apostle Paul, an ardent scholar, to his protégée young Pastor Timothy is a crucial secret to becoming a giant. The surest way of standing head above shoulder among peers in your vocation is to study (develop) to become an expert at your trade. Spare no time, expense and effort in developing your skills and abilities. Only then can one guarantee that the world would beat its path to ones door even if you lived in the wilderness. Without such an aggressive approach to personal development, shame at failing to fulfil one's potential is a sure inevitability.

3. Proverbs 22:29

Seeth thou a man diligent in his business? He shall stand before kings; he shall not stand before mean men.

It was the development and deployment of Joseph's gift of interpretation of dreams and administration that brought him straight from the prison, before Pharaoh and onto become the Prime Minister of Egypt (Genesis 37:5-11;39:2-3,22-3;40 & 41).He was suddenly raised from the prison to the palace on account of developing and utilising his divinely endowed gift. If you too would dare to develop that gift there is no limitations to the heights it would take you.

4. Ecclesiastes 10:16

Woe to you o land, when your king is a child, and your princes feast in the morning.

Indeed unrest, regression, stagnation befalls all organisation in which the ruler, king, director or leader is under developed and without experience like the child appointed King. If you are the lead in your family, business, church or office ensure you do not set a lid over it by your underperformance consequent to under development.

Chapter Five summary

1. Though every human is naturally endowed to be outstanding, choice and personal effort determines level of achievement.

2. The unprocessed natural endowments are like raw precious stones, which require refining for optimal use.

3. Development rather than recognition of talents is a commonly encountered human problem and hindrance to achievement.

4. Natural endowment must be developed for the following reasons

    a. optimisation of benefit of abilities

    b. elimination of regression

    c. lifting the lid over achievement

    d. production of excellence and attraction of reward

5. Self -development may require training, education, tutelage, coaching or mentoring.

6. Giants are those who make a personal choice to develop self

7. Giants assess and make plans to meet their development needs

8. Giants identify resources to meet those needs by assessing content, method and results of resources.

9. Giants convert acquired knowledge into consistent action, which becomes a habit.

10. Giants practice habits of life long learning which is manifested by:

   a. Daily learning

   b. Daily reading

   c. Self scrutiny

   d. Teaching others

   e. Growing from mistakes

   f. Self exposure

   g. Change embracing

   h. Self investment

11. The bible teaches the following lessons:

   Jesus taught that every human has talents that should be developed

One who fails to develop their talent risk being ashamed in their vocation or trade

Personal development would take the talented to great heights as it took Joseph from the prison to the palace

The leader who fails to develop attracts consequences in their area of jurisdiction.

Action plan and reflection

1. Can you list the natural talents and abilities you have?

2. In what specific ways do you need to develop them to achieve your life's goals?

   Write down a SMART goal statement in developing 2 of these abilities.

3. Identify and write down two of the life long learning habits of giants you wish to adopt and when.

4. Memorize one of the self -development scriptures and meditate on it daily through the period of reading this book.

The first and best victory is to conquer self.

Plato. Greek Philosopher

We must all suffer from one of two pains: the pain of discipline or the pain of regret. The difference is discipline weighs ounces while regrets weigh tons.

Jim Rohn, International business philosopher

CHAPTER 6

Discipline Habits of Giants

In our study of giants, we have so far found that their habits are the footprints, which make their lives remarkable and memorable. These habits are formed when a desire to live a life that counts overweighs the lethargy to live in the slow, unchallenging lane of life. However, it is only when such desire to leave a positive legacy is converted into a firm decision backed up by corresponding action that the journey to achievement begins. This journey would not be completed except the potential giant sacrificially develops himself and his abilities to meet with the challenges ahead.

Personal development cannot be achieved without self -discipline and mastery. Discipline is therefore a crucial ingredient in the life style of the giant.

The Cambridge dictionary defines self-discipline as "the ability to make yourself do things you know you should do even when you do not want to".

The American Heritage Dictionary of the English language describes self-discipline as *"Training and control of oneself and one's conduct, usually for personal improvement"*. This definition connotes self- made restriction imposed over a period for purpose of achievement. Discipline is not a one off exercise but a life style and habit of doing that, which is demanded rather than desired. I like the way Bishop David Oyedepo put it-"operating as demanded not as convenient".

Allow me to share with you a few jewels of wisdom on the association of discipline with human achievement and eminence.

Self-Discipline is crucial to personal development

It is rarely the case that an undisciplined person gets to the pinnacle of their endeavours. Should this aberration occur, the achievement is usually transient and marked with a great fall if discipline is not quickly imbibed! No one gets to and stays long at the top without the ability to master his appetites and impulses.

I agree with Tom Hopkins who said if you are not willing to accept your own discipline, you are not going to accomplish two percent of what you could-and you are going to miss out on ninety- eight percent of the good things you could have. If you really mean to be and remain a giant, self-discipline is not negotiable. It is essential in self -development and without self development greatness cannot be unravelled.

Self-discipline is always a personal choice

When it comes to the discipline that takes a person right to the top, this is always a matter of a personal choice rather than coercion. A higher authority could inflict disciplinary actions or castigation on an erring subordinate; however ,the art of mastery of personal appetites and impulses is always a matter of individual choice. No wonder James A Ray commented that "the only competition you will ever have is the competition between your disciplined and undisciplined mind.

Self -discipline can only result form a personal promise to self always to act based on the desired future goal rather than immediate and present gain. To rise early in the day, to put in two extra hours of work daily or commit to at least one hour of study daily rather than waste precious hours being entertained by the soap box can only be the choice of one who is driven. I mean giants who are driven by the internal commitment to personal accountability rather than the external control of human expectation. Self –discipline is always by choice and not chance.

Self-Discipline is painful but profiting.

Let us face it, no one really enjoys restraining the body and the mind. The only motivation at all times is the benefit to be obtained. No matter for how long he has practised the habit, the Olympic marathon gold medallist does not enjoy rising up at five on a winter morning to commence his ten -mile jog for the day. The thought of what the undesirable consequence of failing to train may be on the day of reckoning however gets him out of bed and onto the road.

One could not agree more with James Allen, author of *As A Man thinketh* who cautioned that He who would accomplish little must sacrifice little, he who would achieve much must sacrifice much, he who must attain highly must sacrifice greatly. If your life must count for much you must learn to master the appetite for sleep, food, sex and unlimited leisure or recreation. The giants of our times are those who have achieved the self- mastery of these appetites as well as discipline in their thought, talk, task, time use and practice of tranquility.

The import of discipline in becoming a giant cannot be overemphasised. We according to Jim Rohn, must all suffer from one of two pains: the pain of discipline or the pain of regret. The difference, he says, is that discipline weighs ounces whilst regrets weigh tons. The choice would however always be personal and individual. A decision every one has to make whether to compromise the present and maximise the future or paradise the current and jeopardise the future. The call is yours!

Discipline habits in Thought

Psychologist, William James stated that the greatest discovery of his generation was that human beings could alter their lives by altering their attitude of mind. Indeed one who wishes to join the roll call of giants must live conscious of this discovery. Humans are the product of our thought processes and recurring patterns of rumination. It is a well known law of life that recurrent thoughts would eventually become repeated talk which in turn would result in repeated acts(tasks).These repeated tasks end up in forming a habit and lifestyle that influences the environment. These habits, according to the central message of this book are what determine the future and destiny of humans.

Your thoughts rule your world. What you think means more than anything else in your life. More than what you earn, more than, where you live, more than your social position, and more than what anyone else may think about you. (Author, George Matthew Adams). The bottom line is all of these variables are in essence influenced by what you think. No wonder the bible warns that the heart be guarded with all diligence because out of it flows the issue of life. I am privileged to be the bearer of the good tidings that you can change your outcome by changing your thoughts accordingly.

Your thought pattern is one of the single most potent predictors of your future. One of the reasons leading corporations' world wide take several hours and sometimes days to interview each candidate applying for their top ranking positions is to gain an insight into their thought processes. You cannot lead others except you think like a leader and see yourself as one in your mind's eye. It has been said that if a pauper by some chance stubbles over a windfall of a million pounds but he does not quickly begin to think like and perceive himself as a millionaire, his wealth would disappear in but a little space of time.

How do you see yourself in your organisation, church, business or the society at large? The answer is so crucial since a man can not out perform his own self- perception. Like John Maxwell puts it, *No one can live on a level inconsistent with the way he sees himself.*

Giants are those who have learnt to identify and extinguish self -destructive thought patterns that jeopardize their journey to the top. May I lean on my experience as a psychiatrist to share with you well established negative thought patterns that are detrimental to your upward journey?

Leading American Psychiatry Professor Aaron Beck's discovery in 1960s that mood disorders, particularly depression and anxiety were closely linked to dysfunctional or faulty thought patterns led to a land breaking revolution in the treatment of these conditions. He proposed that *depressive cognitions* consist of *automatic thoughts that reveal negative views of the self, the world, and the future.* The automatic thoughts he believed, were sustained by illogical ways of thinking which he described as *cognitive distortions.*

He found out that if we think some thoughts often enough, we begin to believe them no matter how untrue they were. Then our feelings and subsequently life experiences would, like a processed negative film, begin to match and align with what is coded in the blue print image of our minds.

The whole ethos of Cognitive Behavioural Therapy (CBT),the most versatile form of talking therapy; according to United Kingdom's National Institute of Clinical Excellence(NICE)- is founded on Professor Beck's initial revolutionary discovery.

Faulty thought patterns do not necessarily result in mood problems, but are equally as limiting to ultimately compromise, delay or abolish achievements and personal effectiveness. Here are some of the thought patterns to eliminate if you wish to get to the top and live a life that leaves a positive legacy.

All or Nothing (Black or white) thinking pattern

This is a thought pattern in which there is a tendency to interpret events and situations in an exclusive black or white fashion. It is a ruminating style that never sees the silver lining on the clouds of life's challenges. However the giants of this age are those who can see some good in every event no matter how dismal.

Overgeneralization

Overgeneralization is simply drawing a general conclusion on basis of a single incident. It is the thought style that allows past negative experiences to deter from attempting to seize the challenges and potential victories of the future.

Do you tend to make hasty general conclusions based on isolated events? Perhaps this thought pattern is manifested in writing colleagues off too quickly based on a single act of omission or commission. Prejudices such as racism and ageism are usually the result of this dysfunctional thought pattern. In order to become a giant you must eliminate this limiting thought pattern.

Mental Filter (Selective Abstraction)

This entails focussing on minute details at the detriment of ignoring more important features of a situation. This is the type of thought pattern that makes an eloquent speaker whose presentation aroused a deafening ovation, to focus on the puzzled look he perceived he received from a member of the audience during his speech. He mentally filters out the several indications of a successful performance and focuses on the insignificant detail suggesting displeasure in one member of his audience.

Catastrophic thinking.

Catastrophic thinking always envisages the worst case scenario. It makes hell of a blissful experience and always anticipates the worst possible outcome. It is the thought pattern in those who are always hanging on the edge of a great experience waiting for something to go wrong as usual. Catastrophic thinking makes a mountain out of a mole hill of challenges.

Having considered several destructive thought patterns it is worth giving a consideration to how to achieve a disciplined thought habit and life style. It is crucial to recognise that it is possible to be disciplined in what you allow to reside in your mind and thought arena. You cannot stop dysfunctional thoughts flying through your mind but you can consciously practice eliminating them before they become a recurrent thought that when allowed to thrive births talk and tasks which could mortgage your future. This brings to mind an adage that says *you can not prevent birds flying over your head but you can certainly prevent them perching and building a nest there.*

Negative thoughts are like birds which have the free will to fly into your mind, but whether you entertain them and allow them room to grow and thrive by rumination; is a different ball game. It is helpful to talk out loud or under the breath to counteract and terminate such destructive thought patterns when identified. They would however only ever be identified when there is a conscious effort to impose a censure on what is allowed to reside in the mind.

May I give you this piece of precious advice? The surest way of censuring what comes into your mind is to control what you feed into it via your sense of hearing and sight. The mind, like a computer runs on whatever software it is fed by way of hearing, seeing and feeling. These are the gate keepers to your thoughts .Never believe anyone who tells you what you read, the movies you see or the music you listen to does not matter. Neither science, scripture nor secular experience support this subtly erroneous but powerfully destructive notion. What you think is a function of what you habitually hear, read and see. Giants recognise this secret and jealously guard the gateways to their minds. No wonder the bible warns to guard the heart (thoughts) above all that one guards. Prov 4:23.

The Power of the Human Mind

The mind, human seat of intellect whose functions are controlled by the brain, has been described as the most potent computer system ever. No wonder Earl Nightingale described the human mind as the last great unexplored continent on earth.

The human mind is so powerful. It has the ability to make hell of heaven and heaven of hell. Cognitive Behavioural Scientists tell us that it is not an event in itself that determines outcome, but the interpretation of that event.

Let me use the illustration of a job loss to drive home my point. Happy-the-lucky loses his mundane, unchallenging shop assistant job in an economic recession. He is unhappy his means of livelihood is compromised but embraces this as the opportunity he has always wanted to develop his passion for writing. Rather than spend his time moaning over his loss and job -hunting for another dead end job, he seizes the moment enrols on an evening writer's beginner's course and spends his days in the library writing short character building stories for Children. He has always wanted to publish his children's storybook but never had enough thinking space to put his thoughts into words on paper until he lost his job. Four years on Happy-the-lucky has published five books and his name is fast becoming known in the industry. He generates more income monthly from royalties and related revenues than his annual salary as a sales assistant. The difference to his story came when he chose to see his job loss as an opportunity to develop his passion rather than the permission to be grounded on the doe.

Miss grumpy, Happy-the-lucky's colleague who suffered a similar plight does not have such a successful story. Soon after being laid off ,she slipped into a state of depression and became a recluse shutting herself off from the world. *She would never recover from this economic blow that has been dealt to her in her middle age,* she reckons. Who would employ a middle aged woman with little more than customer care skills in this economic dearth?

Four years on Grumpy is still on state support and contributing nothing to the society. Could somebody please tell Miss Grumpy, middle age is not a plague? Ray Croc's started his now International billion dollar McDonalds empire in his middle age. At the age of 52 he had diabetes, had lost his gall bladder and most of his thyroid gland. Yet his conviction that "the best was ahead of me" flourished and the results speaks for itself today.

How about Colonel Saunders, his rival company who started Kentucky Fried Chicken at his retirement at age 67 when he discovered his pension paycheque left him with a shortfall. Miss Grumpy is only 50 and she does not have to allow life to pass her by because of her job loss.

The Grumpies of the world need to be reminded of the words of the Irish Dramatist and critic George Barnard.

People are always blaming their circumstances for what they are. I don't believe in circumstances. The people who do get on in this world are the people who get up and look for the circumstances they want and if they can't find them-Make them!

Guarding the heart

Guard your heart more than you guard your income, your savings, the house, the diamonds or your ministry! Neither of these is secure until you guard your heart.

Allow me to share with you a few precious thoughts on guarding your heart or practising discipline in your thoughts

Scrutinize your input

If indeed the human mind is a computer, then it stands to good reasoning that the *garbage in, garbage out* information technology principle applies. You cannot spend your time reading celebrity gossip magazines and watching filthy and mundane television and expect that your thoughts would have any quality as such that would take you to the top. You take a closer look at the giants around you and observe what they allow into their hearts.

Practice creative thinking

The mind is such an under utilised tool of human development. At those times when you are not carrying a stimulating book to read on that train journey and your laptop is not with you, have you had a thought about programming your powerful and internal computer. The human mind is such a durable computer system. You don't need extra costs to carry it with you on every journey.

The habit and lifestyle of consciously focussing the mind on developing ideas, concepts and problem solving cannot be under emphasised. I mince no words in saying consciously musing over scriptural verses is a habit I practice as a lifestyle. If you must be a giant in your endeavour then learn to stretch the imagination of your mind by consciously exercising your thoughts on the true, the honest and good thoughts.

It has been said that your worth in life is a product of the use of your mind. The quality of a man's life is determined by the state of his mind.(Bishop David Oyedepo). David Schwartz , best selling author of Magic of Thinking Big put it this way-Where success is concerned, people are not measured in inches, or pounds, or college degrees or family background; they are measured by the size of their thinking. How do you rate yourself in the quality of your thoughts and imaginations?

Counteract negative thoughts

Negative thinking cannot be wished away. Their elimination is always the product of a conscious effort to change the status quo. A sure way of nipping negative thoughts in the bud is either to speak out loud or speak under one's breath, a counteracting statement. Next time you catch yourself thinking those *I'm a total failure, I'll never make it, I haven't got what it takes to get to the top* thoughts; open your mouth wide and speak out loud in the opposite. Don't just seat there and pretend it does not matter whether you let such thoughts fester or not, because it does matter!

Listen and learn from what Robert Kiyosaki said in his *Rich Dad Poor Dad 2* –"*No matter what anyone is saying to you from the outside, the most important conversation is the one you are having with yourself on the inside*". Indeed the most important charter is not the one between two opposing enemies but that between each of their two ears. The dialogue you allow to fester and grow in your mind determines where you end up- as a giant or an ant.

Allow me to share with you a simple secret on how to assess your self -talk. The mind charter (dialogue) which occurs between your temples when you miss your targets in life is a potent indicator of your self- talk. If when you miss, you look at yourself and conclude you knew you were no good anyway, then your self -talk needs a change. If when you miss you reaffirm yourself with the reassuring belief that failing is out of character and unlike your true self then you are on your way to greatness?

The import of self -talk on achieving greatness cannot be overemphasized. Listen to what Brian Tracy, leading Sales and time management consultant has to say about self talk-Ninety five percent of your emotions whether positive or negative are determined by the way you talk to yourself on a minute- to- minute basis.

The story was once told about a folk tale narrated by a witty grandfather to his beloved school age grandson. It was a tale to illustrate the power of the battle of the mind on outcome in life's entire endeavours. Granddad told his grandson a story about two fighting wolves. The battle line was drawn and the outcome of the feud was one of far reaching consequences. It could make pauper of a prince and prince of a pauper. The outcome of this crucial battle of the wolves could make hell of heaven and heaven of hell. It was a battle to be fought to the finish. It was one with grave and lasting consequences.

There were however a few concerns. Both wolves were of equal strength, ability and physique. There was the wolf with the limiting belief and the one with the empowering beliefs. The limiting wolf is the one who always reminds of the thousand and one reasons why a dream cannot be realised. It is the critical, nagging voice that attacks and stifles life out of the project that had the million- pound potential but was never allowed to take off. The empowering wolf on the other hand had his favourite song as "you can if you try". His voice was always there at the times of delays and detours deferring the discouragement.

The grandson was of course more interested in the outcome than the details of the battle. He waited no longer before blurting out " Granddad which wolf won this crucial battle in the end?". The answer was profound and it remains true in our days. It is the wolf you choose to feed! Yes, it is the wolf you take sides with by nurturing and dwelling on their whispers that wins the battle. Your rumination and agreement is what empowers and energises the wolf. The verdict is always yours but only if you know it! Indeed like Henry T Ford put it- "whether you believe you can, or whether you believe you can't, you are probably right". May I ask you which of your wolves you have been feeding? Giants are people who utilise their joker card wisely by carefully feeding the empowering wolf and stifling the limiting one. It is not rocket science. You too can learn to feed your empowering and stifle your limiting beliefs. The choice is yours!

Guard your words

Your words educate your world. That includes yourself and others around you. Your mind is quick to pick up and believe what you keep saying about yourself. You would eventually believe and act on what you keep saying to yourself and others no matter how far from the truth it is.

Discipline Habits in Talk

The second area of discipline giants pays attention to is their talk. Your talk or words are a mirror of your thoughts. You cannot become a giant if you are not disciplined with your talk. It is not so difficult to predict where a man would end up; whether at the top or toped when you listen to them speak. Your words would either get you to the top or top you in your journey to the top. Giants never underestimate the potency of their words in their life's journey. In fact, the giants of our time are those who exploit the power of words in their daily pursuit. Every single day battles of greatness are won and lost with weapons of words. Everyone faces challenges, adversity, set backs and detours in life's journey, but the difference in outcome lies in the manner in which we use our words. Your repeated words either give life and permission or death and termination to the events in your world. That choice to use your words to shape your world would always be yours. How are you using your currency of words?

Allow me to share with you wisdom nuggets about the role of words in taking a man to his throne.

Words are seeds

Words never die or perish, rather they are like seeds, which bring forth their corresponding fruits at maturation. Here are a few things to remember about the seed of words you sow into your life and your world

You reap only if you sow

Giants recognise that words are seeds but there are of no benefit until they are sown into the soil of the heart by verbalisation. The only words that shape your world are those allowed to emerge from the recess of your heart into the tangible perception of hearing.

Giants know the power of professing their desired outcome in the face of contrary and hostile climate. They know words are weapons of war. They speak words of faith and encouragement in the face of defeat and discouragement. They know words are of no benefit until they are verbalised.

Are you exploiting the power of words in your world? When next you confront a challenge, rather than silently ruminate over your inevitable failure, learn to speak words of victory to overcome your challenges. Remember silence is defensive and speaking is offensive in the battle of life.

You reap what you sow

Giants are careful about their words and talk because they realise you reap what you sow. There is no such thing as empty words in the true sense of the word. Words are active, powerful and alive. Words create images. They control thoughts. They paint pictures.

Giants know the secret of seedtime and harvest as far as words are concerned. They know you cannot continue to speak failure and lack and expect a life of success and abundance. They know your words attract its content to your world.

If you were to reap the reward of your words on your health, career, business, marriage, children or ministry, would you like the fruits? If your answer is in contrary, then it's time to change your words.

You reap more than you sow

No matter what faith, creed, colour or country you belong, sowing and reaping is a universal law of life. It applies to all humans.

Great people know that the other reason to be careful about words is that you always reap more than you sow. It takes simply observing a farmer to realise this fundamental truth .He plants a grain of wheat and reaps a stalk or two. He plants a handful of grains and reaps a farmland of harvest. In the same manner your words always bring back more than you sow

You reap after you sow

It is crucial to remember as you embark on using words for war that you reap after you sow. There may not be a dramatic change in circumstance in one day after your words change. Seed maturation is a process and it occurs at a variable period of time. One however must not resort to the previous pattern of using destructive and counter productive words because the reward is not readily seen.

Giants know you reap after you sow and not when you sow. Hence they maintain words of faith despite contrary evidence and climate. Do you keep talking right even when the fruits of faith are delayed? Remember you reap after you sow.

Discipline Habits in Task

Every human being with a normal brain has been equally endowed with two most crucial success precursors- a creative mind and a twenty four- hour day to put it to work. The discipline in thought must be accomplished in the discipline in task (use of the time currency)in order to achieve greatness.

There are several angles to consider when addressing the discipline habits in task. There are however two crucial aspects that inevitably lead to failure and mediocrity if left unaddressed. These are the habits of time management and focus maintenance.

Habit of time management

Greatness cannot be fully expressed until these crucial truths about time is imbibed and practised.

Time is a more essential and crucial success currency than money. Many humans guard their money to the penny but are extremely frivolous with their time. The truth however is time is more precious than money. In fact, it is wise use of your time that guarantees wealth accumulation. The only exchangeable commodity every human is equally endowed with is a twenty- four hour day. It is the manner in which we habitually spend this commodity that determines our eventual worth to our world.

I challenge you to study and scrutinise the use of your time currency in the next one week. Study your use of time at work, business, play and with friends and family. Are there ways in which you may optimise the use of your time better? Are there tasks you currently engage in that can be effectively delegated to others? Are there projects or endeavours you currently spend time on that are irrelevant to your life's purpose and mission? How about people or events in your life that are leeches on your time, and by consequence sabotage your pursuit of greatness? How about multi tasking or converting apparently "dead time" such as commuting time into meaningful use?

Dead time

Dead time is time spent engaged in a physical task that makes it otherwise impossible to engage in another physical task. The most rampant occurrence in our world is time spent commuting. These times do not allow for much physical but create ample opportunity for mental tasks. I cherish my commuting time because it allows me to meditate, listen to audio recordings or read a personal or spiritual development literature.

Brian Tracey, best selling author and time management guru noted an average car owner drives about five hundred to a thousand hours each year. He then boldly declares that *"You can become one of the smartest, most capable, and highest paid people in your field simply by listening to educational audio programmes as you drive around"*. It is for this reason that my car doubles as a spiritual and personal growth library. This is also why I choose corner -end carriage seats to eliminate distractions to study on my commuting train journey to work.

Habit of Focus Maintenance

Thomas Edison was an exceptional man. In fact, he is today credited as one of the most prolific inventors that has ever lived. In his eighty- four years of life he had over a thousand United States patents and equally as many in Europe to his name. Among Edison's land breaking inventions, was the electric bulb, the gramophone and the concept and implementation of electric-power generation and distribution to homes, businesses, and factories.

One would with thought this great inventor had mental capabilities that were beyond those of the average man. However, by his own confession when asked the secret of such as a productive life his response was that whilst many men spend their time focussing on several things over the course of the day, he spends his focussing on just one thing that was the matter at hand. Do you focus on the task at hand or you are a Jack of all trade and a master of none?

80/20 Rule of Time

In 1906 Italian economist Vilfredo Pareto used a mathematical formula to describe his observation that 80 percent of his country's wealth was possessed by 20 percent of the population. In the course of time, this concept became popular and was found to be universally applicable and true in many other spheres of human endeavours. The ideology was later reinforced by Dr Joseph Juran, Quality management pioneer who worked in the 1940s when he described it with the "vital few and trivial many" phrase. It was Juran who then attributed the 80/20 principle to Pareto; hence the alternative term Pareto's Principle.

The 80/20 rule is simply that 20 percent of tasks are always responsible for 80 percent of results. Time management consultants have believed for several years that an effective time manager is one who finds the 20 percent of the activity that is crucial and responsible for 80 percent of his output and concentrates on these vital few tasks. He then devotes 80 percent of his time on this crucial 20 percent tasks that generate 80 percent of his output.

A giant is one who has identified his or her vital few tasks and contends to stay focussed on them without being distracted into majoring in the minor of the trivial many. He has mastered the game of devoting his best time resource and energy on the crucial tasks. Now, the relevant question here is; can the giant who is currently reading these words optimise their own greatness even more, by identifying and focussing on their vital few by relegating their trivial many? Can he devote 80 percent of his best resources towards 20 percent of his vital few tasks that generate the 80 percent of his outcome?

Famous focus Quotes

The import of focus on achievement cannot be over emphasized. It has been said that *the sunrays do not burn until it is brought to a focus* (Alexander Graham Bell, renowned inventor and engineer).

Orison Swett Marden, nineteenth century author, and founder of the internationally reputed American Business motivational *Success magazine*; puts his thoughts on focus as thus-"*Every man has become great, every man has succeeded in proportion as he has confined his powers to one particular channel*".

The weakest living creature, by concentrating his powers on a single object can accomplish something, whereas the strongest, by dispersing his over many, may fail to accomplish anything. (Thomas Carlyle)

Success is like a postage stamp; its usefulness depends on its ability to stick to one thing until it gets there. (Dr Bill Newman, Australian author and preacher)

Concentrate on what you do well and do it better than anybody else-John Schnatter, founder of Papa John Pizza

When we aim at everything, we shall hit nothing- Dr Myles Munro, Preacher, best selling author and International motivational speaker.

Personalising focus

It is impossible to leave a mark on time until you learn to focus your efforts on your task and life's purpose. According to Bishop David Oyedepo, "more often than

not only those who live for one thing become outstanding"
The world's reward system has always favoured those
who distinguish themselves in a particular field of human
endeavour. You think about it, how many professorial
seats, Nobel prizes, Grammys, OBEs and Oscars are
awarded without specifying the niche area? None!

Are you focussed in your pursuits? Do you get easily
distracted and derailed? Are you a good finisher of tasks
or a collector of incomplete projects? If indeed, you wish
to be great you need to find what you've been called to
do and remain focussed on doing it until you leave a
mark on time.

If you have found you are not one to complete tasks, it
is pertinent to examine why this is the case. What is your
most potent distraction that prevents you from carrying
through with initiated projects? Are you one who always
seeks novelty at the altar of sacrificing completion? Or
is it about giving up too soon when facing obstacles and
challenges. Let me encourage you, there is no achiever in
life who did not have enough opportunities and reasons
to give up on their tasks. Everyone who achieved much
did so because they refused to be detracted from their
passion until they saw desirable outcome. If you wish
to join that roll of honours, you need to persevere with
your task.

I was fascinated to learn after reading and getting
inspired by Denis Waitley's *Psychology of Winning* that he

had kept the manuscript of that book in the shelf for five years because he believed it was no good. Eventually it emerged out of the shelf, heralded Mr Waitley's arrival on the American motivational speaking scene and spurred him on to become leading Olympic coach and winning consultant. He was head of Psychology of the American Olympic Team for several years. *Psychology of winning* has since become a leading motivational audio programme world wide, having been translated into over a dozen languages. How about if Mr Waitley had not persevered on his project?

Discipline habits in Tranquillity.

My observation after a keen study is that the winning actors in the stage of life are those who ever so frequently dare to step back stage to reappraise their role, the stage and their audience. These giants are bold enough to part with the fun fare for a moment to refine their movement.

It is sad to note that many today are running on the track of life but have forgotten what they are chasing. They are akin to the man on the treadmill machine who is working hard without evidence of advancement. They are caught in the motion and moving ever so fast to the increasing rhythm of the twenty first century beat. They are oblivious of their origin and destination, caught in the rat race trying to save face rather than take a break.

Tranquillity has become a luxury in our contemporary world where silence is alien and almost extinct. Those who are giants in their field however still cherish solitude and tranquillity. The blessings of planned purposeful periods of stepping back to rethink cannot be overemphasised if one must achieve and maintain greatness. Solitude and tranquillity of mind is inevitably accompanied by a physical, mental and spiritual refreshing crucial to sustainability. Most land breaking ideas and concepts are born at periods of retreating from the maddening crowd of life with a view to re-fire.

Life lessons from Eagles.

I am an advocate and devotee of regular spiritual and physical retreats. I have learnt from the eagles that wait in solitude until their strength is renewed. One of the remarkable and self -preserving attributes of the eagle is its ability to renew its youth. It is believed that eagles have a life span of up to seventy years. However, in their mid life they must undergo a process of rejuvenation or moulting if they are to survive the latter half.

Usually in their forth decade of life the eagles would have lost their agility and hunting prowess. The feathers which were otherwise flexible for swift and highflying would have become soiled with dirt and oil making it heavy and stuck to the eagle's trunk. Their talons (claws) and beaks loses it's sharpness as a result of calcium deposition. These changes render the eagle an ineffective hunter and may result in untimely death by starvation if not addressed. Calcification of the beak also results in the head of the king of the skies becoming weighed down and bowed in despondency.

It is at such times that the eagle isolates itself to the top of mountain where they undergo the solitary process of moulting. They patiently and repeatedly strike first their talons against the hard rock until it is shed off completely. They then wait until it grows back and repeat the process with the shedding of their beaks and completely stripping their feathers. The eagle then washes itself in a river to rid any further dirt and pollutant. This sometimes-difficult process has been known to last up to five months during which the eagle is vulnerable and waits patiently to re-grow its beak, talons and feathers whilst it basks in the sunshine to keep warm. It is not unusual for them to depend on colleagues who have undergone a similar process to feed them at this time of vulnerability and ineffectiveness.

The eagle after completing moulting returns to the high sky with renewed vitality, fresh sharp talons and beaks and re-grown strong wings equipped for effectiveness. It is now able to support other eagles that may in the future undergo the process.

The giants in life know that no matter your height of greatness and achievement you need regular periods of retreat in order to refine and refocus your vision. It is a time to get rid of the dirt and oils of limiting beliefs and associations, which has been acquired over time. They value such seasons when they retire to re-fire. They welcome this opportunity to raise a head that is bowed down in frustration of unfulfilled dreams and unrealised goals. The giants who do not recognise or respond to the need for the moulting process required in tranquillity and solitude are never around for long enough to leave a mark on their time. They, like the eagle that remains in the sky despite failing strength and agility eventually succumb to an untimely death.

May I ask you whether tranquillity and solitude ever finds a place in your busy overbooked diary? There are ample lessons to be learnt from the eagles.

It is suffice to conclude and tie the discipline in talk, thought, task and tranquillity together by quoting Joseph McClendon III- "Life is a canvas, your imagination (*thoughts*) is the paint and your activity (*tasks*) is the paint brush. Dip your brush into the paint of your desire and dare to paint of your life a master piece".

What the bible says about discipline

Discipline is a mark of greatness

Proverbs 16:32

He that is slow to anger is greater than the mighty and he that ruleth his spirit is greater than he that takes a city.

Discipline is required in obtaining an excellent outcome

1 Corinthians 9:27

But I put my body under (discipline) lest after I have preached unto others I myself become a cast away (unaccepted, rejected or failure).

Self denial /discipline is an emblem of discipleship

Matthew 16:24

Then Jesus said to his disciples If any man would follow me, let him deny (discipline) himself, take up his cross and follow me

Discipline of thought is crucial to life success

Proverbs 4:23

Guard your heart with all diligence for out of it are the issues of life.

The New Century version gives more insight by stating *Be careful what you think, your thoughts run your life.*

Your thoughts rule your world

Proverbs 23:7

a For as he thinks in his heart so he is.

External manifestation results from internal transformation

Romans 12:1

Do not be conformed to this world but be transformed by the renewing of your mind that you may prove the acceptable will of God.

Your words rules your world

Proverbs 18:20

A man shall be satisfied with good by the fruit of his mouth and by the recompense of his words shall he be rewarded.

Mark 12:37

By your words, you would be justified and by your words, you would be condemned.

Diligence precedes greatness

If you see a man who is diligent in his works (tasks) he shall stand before kings and not mere(common) men.

Time must be accurately discerned and utilised

Ecclesiastes 3:1

there is a time and a season for every purpose under heaven.

God gives spiritual, physical and mental renewal and restoration during periods of tranquillity.

Isaiah 40:31-

They that wait upon the Lord shall renew their strength, they shall mount up with wings as eagles, they shall run and not be weary, they shall walk and not faint.

Psalm 103:5

Who (the Lord) satisfies thy mouth with good things and renews your youth as that of eagle

Chapter Six summary

1. Discipline is operating as demanded not as convenient.

2. Self-discipline is crucial to achieving personal development

3. Self discipline is always a personal choice.

4. Self discipline is painful but profitable

5. Human beings can alter our life by altering the attitude of our minds

6. Your thoughts rule your world and is a potent predictor of your future.

7. Psychiatrists and psychologists have identified recurring patterns of thoughts that result in mood problems. These dysfunctional thought patterns also sabotage greatness.

8. The surest way to control what resides in your thought is to control what you hear and see.

9. The mind is the human's powerful computer system that operates based on the software of thoughts it is fed.

10. An adverse event in itself is not as harmful as the negative interpretation of it. Men of note in history have through a positive interpretation

of personal adverse events become giants in their own rights.

11. No asset is secured until the human heart (mind) has been securely guarded. The heart can be guarded by scrutinizing input, practicing creative thinking and counteracting negative thoughts.

12. Battles of greatness are fought and lost on the field of words.

13. Words are proverbial seeds. You reap only if, what, more than and after you sow them.

14. Time management and focus maintenance must be mastered before greatness is achieved.

15. Giants apply the 80/20 rule of focussing their best resources of time and energy on the vital few tasks crucial for their greatest outcomes.

16. What the bible says about discipline, thoughts, talk and tasks.

  a.   Discipline is a marker of greatness

  b.   Discipline is a pre requisite to obtaining an excellent outcome.

  c.   Discipline is an emblem of true discipleship

d. Discipline is crucial to life success

e. Your thoughts and words rule your world

f. External manifestation is always the result of internal transformation

g. Diligence precedes greatness.

Action plan and reflection

1. How disciplined are you in your thought, talk and tasks?

2. In which one area of your life do you need to change your talk in order to achieve different outcomes?

3. Evaluate your thoughts with a view to identifying the single most recurring dysfunctional thought pattern that has sabotaged your greatness.

   Apply the remedies proposed.

4. Evaluate your task and compile a list of the vital few tasks. Identify and list those trivial many tasks you would relegate or delegate.

Self -esteem is believing that you have the potential to be a world- class person irrespective of current performance

-Denis Waitley,
Author Psychology of Winning.

The fist step towards success is believing in yourself, believe you can succeed

- David Schwartz, Author
The Magic of Thinking Big

CHAPTER 7

Discernment Habits of Giants

The Cambridge advanced learners dictionary defines discernment as the ability to judge people and things well. Its counterpart the Compact Oxford English dictionary describes its root word discerning as having or showing good judgement. In order to become a giant in your field and in life you cannot do without the benefit of good and sound judgement. Every one who has left a mark on the sand of time have had to develop and utilise good judgement both as a daily skill and a deciding one at the cross roads of their lives.

There are several spheres in which giants exercise discernment, notable among them are

1. Discernment of personal worth and value

2. Discernment of personal strengths and weaknesses

3. Discernment of personal associations and relationships; and

4. Discernment of opportunities for greatness.

Discernment of personal worth and value.

It has been said that abuse is inevitable when value is not rightly discerned. I dare say that no one can embark on the journey to greatness and significance until they settle once and forever the notion in their hearts that they are beings of immense value and worth to their world. Allow me to be the bearer of great tidings that no matter your age, race, physique, social background, or country of residence; you carry in you a gold mine of priceless value to your world.

I encourage you to celebrate your rarity and uniqueness. There is no shame or pride in thinking there is no one exactly like you in the whole planet. For starters, though there are six billion humans on earth, no one shares your unique genetic coding reflected by your biometric data. No matter who you are or are not, you have every reason to celebrate your individuality. No one else on earth shares your unique blend of physique, socioeconomic background, temperament, internal and external preferences. You are the only original version of the brand "ME". Become accustomed and comfortable with your style and cease being apologetic for being you.

Do not let anyone put you down or demean your value. It has been said that no one can make you feel inferior without your permission. You are an asset to your world and until you see yourself as such, you would not manifest your full potential of greatness.

Allow me to share with you my unique experience of individuality. I am one of those rare and privileged humans who have an exceptionally identical twin. Only 0.2 percent (two in a thousand) of the world population are identical twins. Furthermore, the genetic similarity with my twin brother is heightened by the fact that we are among an even rarer 1-2 percent of identical twins who shared the same placenta and birth sac. Our striking similarity is such that only our beloved mother and our own off springs can boast of never have fallen into the error of mistaken our identity at one point or the other. Yet, despite our uncommon genetic similarity, we are both unique in our individual rights, appreciate and relish our similarity, but equally celebrate our differences and individuality.

Dr Ben Carson, internationally acclaimed Paediatric Neurosurgeon reputed for pioneering the first successful surgical separation of cephalic conjoined twins; said- *"There is no such thing as an average human being. If you have a normal brain you are superior"*. Who else is better disposed to make such an assertion after rising from being the bottom of his primary school class to becoming an internationally acclaimed neurosurgeon.

Indeed, you are superior and no matter who you are, the world can be a better place for your unique contribution; but only if you stand up to be counted in.

You do not have to be a world- class person right now, but you must believe you have the potential like everyone else to become one.

The Magic in Ideas

I would like to share with you one of the most profound thoughts in this book .Grasping this concept has enriched my own life in no small measure. And it is that-Giants place very high esteem and value on their own ideas. They take very seriously the ideas that pop into their minds in the midst of their busy daily schedule.

What is an idea then? It is simply a notion or thought conceived in the mind. Every product, service or system that is of immense benefit to the human race today started as an idea in somebody's mind. From laser surgery to facebook, space travel, airplanes, solar energy and the ipod, all are products of an idea that a giant dared to bring from the realm of their thought into tangible world by faith-filled action. The great song of encouragement, the beautiful painting, award- wining movie, and inspirational book were all once in the realm of somebody's thought until they took them serious enough to act. If you really want to live an exceptional life, I encourage you to value your ideas.

Ideas are powerful. They are the seeds of what life eventually becomes. Let me share with you an analogy on ideas. Ideas are like egg cells in the ovary of a baby girl. At birth, every girl is born with a million egg cells in each of her two ovaries. Every one of these eggs has the potential to become a full term healthy living baby if exposed to the right condition. By the time of puberty, the number of eggs would have been depleted to only forty thousand. At each menstrual cycle, several of these potential baby precursors go through a maturation process, but only one of them succeed to the phase of being released into the woman's tube in anticipation for meeting the male sperm. Even then, a release of the successful egg does not guarantee conception as timing of intercourse is crucial. Eventually over a woman's reproductive life span, only about four hundred eggs are released of which, for many women there are two to four life births on the average.

Ideas are like human eggs with countless of them flooding the human mind daily and over an entire lifetime, but only very few captured and harnessed to better human state. Achievers do not play with their ideas. Here are eight ways by which giants harness the benefit from their ideas.

Record Ideas

Great men value their ideas enough to record them as promptly and verbatim as possible. I have been keeping a journal of my ideas and life experiences for a while and the benefits are priceless. I was not surprised to read Sir Richard Branson, the billionaire head of the Virgin group of companies, confession that many of the ideas that brought him his stupendous wealth were initially captured on pieces of scrap or tissue paper. No wonder he said "Ideas can emerge at anytime, anywhere and often when you are least expecting them. It's what we create with these ideas that can make a difference to all our lives. With that difference reward can follow"

The great and noble ensure they are not caught off guard by carrying recording materials with them as a habit. It is worth developing the habit of carrying a recording device be it electronic or manual. I am rarely without easy reach of a pen and jotter except when in bed. It has been said that a short pencil is sharper than the longest memory. Writing down ideas confers additional benefit of clarification and ease of communication to others. Do not rely on your memory, rather form the winning habit of recording your ideas and thoughts as promptly and accurately as possible with the date and context clearly indicated. David Schwartz in *The Magic of Thinking Big* said-"Ideas are perishable, everyday lots of good ideas are born only to die quickly because they aren't nailed to paper".

Research Ideas

To research is to re search, that is, to search over and again with a view to finding. It takes a great mind to research around ideas to convert into a beneficial service, product or system. Some ideas are recorded but never take off because they were not thoroughly researched. Great men do their homework well. These days researching ideas could not be easier with the information overload that the internet age allows.

Review ideas

How many land breaking notions today remain locked up in the pages of notebooks in which they were recorded. Let me ask you, when you take notes at a seminar, in church or in class, how soon after do you return to review and muse over your notes? Sometimes life changing concepts only emerge in the process of reviewing recorded ideas.

Retain Ideas

The world can be very hostile and unsympathetic of new ways or methods of working or thinking. The high and noble know not to give up on their conviction about an idea only because it is not popular. The story of Jeff Bezos, the brain behind the exceptionally successful world's largest internet store *Amazon* comes to mind. Hear his success story in his own words-"Every well-intentioned, high-judgement person we asked told us not to do it". He followed his conviction and the results speak for themselves. Perhaps, you bought your copy of this book from Amazon! Do not let the contrary opinion of others rob you of your million- pound idea. Follow your heart!

Refine Ideas

Many ideas are conceived in the mind in raw version. They are born in unrefined form akin to gold ore that needs purification to bring out its value and beauty. You must learn to refine your ideas to conform to the findings of your research. One of the most versatile and quintessential modern day clothing was the product of such refining of idea.

Levi Strauss was born in Bavaria, Germany. He relocated to New York with his family in his teenage years and later followed the gold rush to the west coast of San Francisco. He had travelled to California with some products he planned to sell to raise investment capital to invest into gold. He had been approached for business partnership by Jacob Davis, a Nevada tailor who had been one of his customers. Jacob had a unique business idea of making durable work pants reinforced at pressure points with metal for strength. He needed a partner to bankroll the patenting of his idea. The resulting partnership evolved into the Levis Jeans. It is no wonder Mr Strauss did not need to invest in gold thereafter.

Relish Your ideas

Relish your ideas enough to guard them. Pacesetters treasure their ideas enough to protect them. Be careful who you discuss your ideas with. Guard your treasure from thieves who could run away with them and discouragers who would talk you out of them. Be wise do not cast your pearls before swine!

Run With Ideas

There is no gain except your run with your ideas. Conrad Hilton, Leader of the Hilton Hotels Empire said- "Success seems to be connected with action. Successful people keep moving. They make mistakes, but they don't quit". Brian Tracy, renowned time management expert reinforced same message in his *Eat that Frog* when he wrote- "For you to achieve any kind of success execution is everything". Simply put the key to success in any realm or endeavour is action. Paul McKenna, best selling author of I can make you rich, had these wise words to share about action-"*Action is a great equalizer. No matter what your level of intelligence, education or capital, a willingness to take massive action instantly puts you on an equal footing with the wealthiest men and women in the world.*"

Let me ask you, what actions are you taking on that idea of improving your productivity, expanding your sphere of influence or increasing your church congregants?

Recycle Your ideas.

Who says ideas cannot be recycled? In my study of opinion leaders and from personal experience, I have discovered the benefit of recycling ideas. Achievers never run out of ideas because they know how to maximise benefit from a single idea or area of strength.

Allow me to share a personal experience of wringing maximum benefit from ideas. A couple of years ago in compliance with my mandatory continuing professional development requirements I took an online educational module on accurate medical recording keeping. I was so impacted by this module that I not only improved the quality of my note taking but also researched the subject further and gave a seminar to share ideas with colleagues. The success of the seminar motivated me even further to write around the same theme in a leadership and management work based project I completed soon after. Needless to say, I completed the course with outstanding performance. By this time, I had realised how crucial and topical my concept was so I wrote an article for publication in my local Psychiatric journal with a view to share benefits and knowledge with an even wider audience. It was a hit with the Editor.

The benefit from a single idea on improving clinical record keeping ranged for improving clinical practice, to obtaining Continuing Professional Development credits, sharing knowledge, improving teaching and publication profile; and obtaining a high profile Leadership Management qualification. Glean all you can from an idea before discarding it. Some of your already discarded ideas may still have much to offer you and others if you would revisit them.

Discernment of Personal Strengths and Weaknesses.

There is no hiding from the reality that all humans are made up of a blend of strengths and weaknesses. The people who excel in life are those who have taken a careful inventory of their skills, talents and personal attributes and learnt to use their discovery to their advantage.

Great men have learnt the craft of focussing on their strengths and compensating for their weaknesses. Rev Matthew Ashimolowo, Pastor of the largest single congregation in UK put it this way- "You never grow into significance if you build your life around your weakness. You only grow into significance when you build your life around your strength".

Let me share with you an advice that could save your future- stop focussing on your weakness. It can be crippling but does not have to be if you know how to handle them. Everyone has them. Humans were not created to be omnipotent but dependent on the omnipotent. What you need to do is to identify, analyse and compensate for your weaknesses. Compensation may entail training and development or delegation of role. However, there are weaknesses you should never bother to improve on because you never can. Exceptional achievers save themselves the heartache of trying to major in the minor areas and minor in the major areas of strength. Save yourself the frustration of low productivity, wasted energy, time and resources that those who try to excel in the areas they are not gifted suffer from.

The lion is the king of the jungle only because it recognises its weaknesses' and uses this to his advantage. Do you know that lions are poor long distance runners despite their imposing and threatening physique? An average lion rests up to twenty hours a day conserving energy and stamina for that short burst run of the day to attack his prey and provide him food until the next meal is due. To ensure a short chase, they use the advantage of factors that reduce visibility such as cover or darkness to sneak as close as a hundred feet to their prey before launching an attack. They then use their strength in powerful jaws and paws, to suffocate their victim.

Giants identify and refine their areas of strength by constant use and practice. They continually seek out opportunities to use their gifts and talents even sometimes at the expense of foregoing remuneration by offering free services. They focus on the long- term gain of cultivating, developing and advertising their gifts rather than short -term benefit of monetary gain.

Every human was born with unique natural abilities and gifting. Your disarming smile, ability to stay calm under pressure, negotiation skills, beautiful soprano voice and aptitude for combining colours are all natural endowments that could take you to your high places if properly cultivated. How about the aptitude for computers, musical instruments or your flare for learning languages?

Mr Tony Blair following his successful tenure of office as British Prime Minister is today earning himself a fortune as a roving World Peace Ambassador because he capitalises on his strength as a great negotiator and persuasive communicator. Let me ask you, what have you got to offer your world? No human was born with nothing. You may not realise it, but there are countless admirers who desire that personal attribute you despise as "nothing".

Find and Count your blessings no matter the cost. If it means asking friends and family, speaking to your pastor, making a personal inventory or taking a psychometric test, make sure you identify and cultivate your strengths. What do you do and get results in effortlessly? What makes you jump out of bed before daybreak and keeps you awake into the early hours? What are you passionate about? That one thing that you do and enjoy doing even when there is no monetary gain. It satisfies your deep longings and gives you a sense of satisfaction no man can comprehend.

What time of the day are you at your peak performance? How about your natural habitat in which you tend to flourish like a fish in water? Who are those in your life who bring out the best in you? Let me share with you a secret great men use to their advantage. They know where you are determines what grows in you. If you stay in the wrong geographical location, it is your weaknesses rather than your strengths that come to the fore. So they are careful where they expend their energy. They never accept every invitation. I encourage you to find answers to these soul-searching questions. Your flying or falling depends on them.

Discernment of personal associations and relationships.

It has been rightly said that you would remain the same way you are today in five years except for two things; the books you read and the people with whom you walk. It is my earnest desire, prayer and expectation that reading the *Footprints of Giants* would feature in your future success story. Now let's talk about personal associations and relationships which either make or mare you.

In my view, there are three groups of healthy relationships that you need in order to flourish into greatness. These are parents, peers and protégées.

Parents are not necessarily biological but in form of mentors who have been where you are headed and can help you to get there quicker, easier and safely. Isaac Newton, renowned physicist said "if I have seen farther, it is because I am standing on the shoulder of those who have gone before me".

The role of mentors in unleashing and nurturing the seed of greatness you carry can never be overemphasized. Save yourself unnecessary detours and delays in your life's journey by seeking out Godly men and women to mentor you. Pray that God would send them into your life.

What is the recipe to finding a great mentor one may ask? Here are Dr Sola Fola-Alade's criteria for finding mentors as outlined in his book *Discover Your Hidden Treasures.*

Attitude- Is your mentor's attitude worth catching?

Belief-What does he believe in? Does he believe in you?

Character- Does he have integrity? Does he practice what he preaches?

Development- Does he develop you?

Experience- Does he have the right kind of experience?

Fruitfulness- does he have results to show for his experiences?

Growth- Is he still growing?

Peers are your contemporaries, friends or colleagues. You need ones who are not jealous of you, motivate, regard but also can correct you in love. Beware if those in your circle of friends are only those who can learn from you but cannot give much to you. I was intrigued to read from Dr Myles Munro's *Principles and Power of Vision* his account of how he sometimes overcomes seasons of discouragement. He would usually telephone his peers and simply ask them about the things God was currently doing in their lives. As they begin to narrate their story, he receives encouragement to rise up and carry on living his own dreams.

No matter how small or great you are every human encounter such seasons when you feel like throwing in the towel on your dreams and settling for less. You need friends who can affirm you and speak encouraging words into your life at such times. If you do not have them ask God to send them into your life and be on the lookout for the answer to your prayers.

Protégées- Who does not need them? They are those to whom you hand over the baton to carry on the legacy when your life's work is done. My heart bleeds when I see several apparently successful men and women who are too busy staying on top than to cultivate a conscious habit of grooming those below them to take over their role at the fullness of time. I could not agree more with the wit who said a success without a great successor is an ultimate failure. It takes time, effort and resources to develop others below you, but it is never a wasted investment. Achievers who wish to have a lasting legacy have learnt the secret of creating time to nurture the seeds of greatness in their subordinates and juniors. Do not let your legacy end with you, invest yourself in greater men who would replicate and synergize your achievements.

Discernment of Opportunities for greatness.

Opportunities can be elusive. Many times, they come masqueraded as insurmountable challenges. It takes a discerning person to see the booty beyond the battle and seize the moment. It has been said that "out of every adversity comes an equal or greater opportunity"(Glenn Bland).

My thoughts are drawn to the lessons from the life of Michelangelo, renowned Italian renaissance sculptor and architect whose work is still celebrated today as outstanding seven centuries on. Michelangelo's marble sculpture of the biblical king *David* is known as one of his most remarkable piece of work. History however records that the same marble from which this renaissance masterpiece was carved had been rejected as too soft by two different reputable sculptors' several years earlier. Michelangelo however saw the David rather than the softness of the marble.

How do you read this next sentence? *Opportunity is nowhere.* Depending on your perception, some read the last phrase as now here whilst others read it as no where. What do you see in your current challenges in marriage, parenting, ministry or your career? Look well enough there may be an opportunity cloaked under the guise of challenges.

Many aspiring achievers moan about the paucity of opportunities. The reality is that opportunities never come to those who wait but they are captured by those who dare to act. Bishop David Oyedepo said "people who think they are too big to do little things are perhaps too little to be asked to do big things". Small opportunities are often the beginning of great enterprises. Smallness is the sure foundation for greatness. Treat every opportunity like it's one of a lifetime. Do your best always. Aim for excellence whether you are attending to a prince or a pauper. Be it in the prison or in the palace. If Joseph, the Dreamer had taken lightly his opportunity to interpreter the prisoner's dreams he may never have been called to the Pharaoh's palace where he became head of government.

What the bible says about personal value, strengths, weaknesses; and relationships and opportunities

Humans are uniquely endowed creatures

Psalms 139:14

I will praise you for I am fearfully and wonderfully made. The Holman's Christian Standard bible says it in plainer language this way- I will praise you, because I have been remarkably and wonderfully made. Your works are wonderful, and I know [this] very well.

God values every human He created

John 3:16

For God so loved the world that he gave his begotten son that whosoever believes in him should not perish but have eternal life.

Christians should be distinguished on earth

1Peter 2:9

But you are a chosen generation, a royal priesthood, a holy nation, a peculiar people to show forth the praises of him who has called you out of darkness into his marvellous light.

Evaluation of personal attributes is crucial to success

Luke 14:28 & 31

For which of you, intending to build a tower, does not sit down first and count the cost whether he has enough to finish it.

Or what king going to war against another king does not sit down first and consider whether he is able with ten thousand to meet him who comes against him with twenty thousand.

Your associations could make or mare you

Proverbs 13:20

He who walks with wise men would be wise but the companion of fools would be destroyed.

Wise associations enhances output

Proverbs 27:17
(Contemporary English Version)

Just as iron sharpens iron; friends sharpen the mind of each other.

Jesus was a mentor

Matthew 4:19

Follow me and I would make you fishers of men.

Faithfulness in small things leads to promotion

Matthew 25:23

His lord said unto him, well done, good and faithful servant: you have been faithful over a few things, I will make you ruler over many things. Enter into the joy of your Lord.

Luke 16:11-12
(New International Reader's Version)

Suppose you have not been worthy of trust in handling worldly wealth. Then who will trust you with true riches? 12 Suppose you have not been worthy of trust in handling someone else's property. Then who will give you property of your own?

Chapter Seven Summary

1. Discernment is the ability to judge people and things well or showing or having good judgement.

2. For a person to become great, rightly esteeming their own personal worth, strengths / weaknesses , associations and opportunities is very crucial.

3. Each person on earth is a creature of rare and unique blend of personal attributes. Celebrate yourself!

4. Great people put a high premium on their own ideas.

5. Ideas when backed with faith-filled action could be translated into tangible products, services and systems that improve human existence.

6. Ideas are perishable. In order to preserve and obtain life changing benefits from them; they should be recorded, researched, reviewed and retained. Ideas should also be refined, relished, run with and recycled for optimal benefit.

7. Each human is a unique blend of personal strengths and weaknesses. Great men focus on their strengths and manage their weaknesses.

8. In order to excel you must identify, cultivate, and regularly use your personal gifting and talents.

9. All aspiring successful people need three crucial relationships-Parents (mentors), Peers (Friends/ associates) and protégées (mentees)

10. Mentors help to achieve greatness easier, quicker and safer. Peers encourage at seasons of discouragement and protégées preserve a legacy of greatness.

11. Most lifetime opportunities to excel come masked as insurmountable challenges.

12. What the bible says about personal worth, strength, weakness, associations and opportunities

   (12.1) Humans are uniquely endowed and divinely valued creatures

   (12.2) Christians should live distinguished lives.

   (12.3) Evaluation of personal attributes is crucial to success

(12.4) Personal associations could make or mare an individual.

(12.5) Jesus was a mentor

(12.6) Faithfulness in small things leads to promotion.

Action plan and Reflections

1. Write down five of what you consider your greatest personal strengths and weaknesses.

2. Identify one area of your strength you wish to cultivate and develop for the next six months. Outline steps you need to take to achieve this goal.

3. Identify two areas of weakness that you wish to manage in the same time frame. Prayerfully decide how to manage this weakness either by training, development or role delegation.

4. Make a formal review of your associations. Write down who you have got as mentors, peers and mentees. Do they meet the criteria of leading you to your desired destination? Prayerfully review this crucial circle of your relationship.

5. Ruminate to identify all the current masked opportunities for greatness, excellence or increase in your life. Ask the Lord to open your eyes to see them and help you to maximise them.

Acorns become oak trees only if they are planted and nurtured

Dr T Ayodele Ajayi

Talent is cheaper than table salt. What separates the talented individual from the successful one is a lot of hard work

- Stephen King

CHAPTER 8

Diligence Habits of Giants

Achievers know talents, giving; praying and great associations cannot substitute or compensate for diligent work. Those who leave unique mark on their world embrace hard work. They habitually practice diligence, which is simply the art of being constant in their application of effort. It means being industrious and failing to excuse lack of perseverance. We live in a quick- fix microwave age in which potential men of substance are quick to abandon their pursuits. We get so easily swayed and misguided by the skin- deep celebrity achieving- without- effort fallacy. Here is how Darren Hardy Editor of cutting edge Success Magazine puts it-

Don't let Hollywood's artificial contrast reference point falsify the reality of what it really takes to be successful: simple, consistent, planned, prepared, and skilled discipline applied every day, compounded over time, accumulating to great success, happiness and prosperity.

Diligence simply put is working hard, well and long enough to produce desired outcome. Here are lessons that I have learnt from scriptures and great men and which I apply in my own life

1. Great men start work.

2. Great men work hard.

3. Great men work on.

4. Great men work smart.

5. Great men work with passion

Great men start work

Whatever you can do or dream you can, begin it. Boldness has genius, power and magic in it. Acorns only ever become oak trees if they are planted and nurtured. The giant of our days know the power and genius associated with starting. If you really want to achieve much you must begin somewhere. The secret to getting ahead is getting started. You are only guaranteed an arrival if you start the journey first. The journey of a thousand miles always begins with that first step. We would never arrive at that beautiful island except we are willing to leave the comfort and safety of our current shore. All great products, services, ministries and systems in our world began small. There is no greatness without the preceding days of small beginnings.

Disney world which today has three sites namely in China, Florida and Paris began in Walt Disney's garage. Walt and his older brother Roy's investment capital was a $500 loan. Their empire today has annual revenue of $35billion. Learn a lesson from Disney. They might have waited forever if they were expecting to start on full potential. My experience is that sometimes until you step out and take action the resources you need may never show up. It seems to me that there are resources out there but they are only attracted to starters.

There is energy in starting. Stop giving yourself lame excuses. Everyone who achieved great things had plausible reasons not to. Helen Keller had the dual whammy of being blind and deaf yet she was first of her kind to obtain a university degree. She went on to pioneer land breaking methods of teaching those similarly disabled, was a prolific author and influential political activist. Beethoven maintained his outstanding musical career despite progressive hearing loss from his late twenties. Sir Winston Churchill had a speech impediment. He overcame this setback to lead Britain as Prime Minister through the Second World War, was a renowned orator and only leader to win a Nobel Prize for Literature.

Start the work today. One today is worth two tomorrows. Enrol on that course. Write that song or book. Launch your website. Start the blogging network. Write your business plan. Register that charity and open that orphanage. Only starters finish. My final word on starting is that you cultivate the habit of marking your starting point. Celebrate your beginnings in anticipation of the desired end. Start with the knowledge that the end is bright. Beginnings are worth celebrating because it takes faith and effort to overcome the inertia of the status quo.

Great men work hard.

The next lesson in diligence is to work hard. In the real world, only hard workers have lasting achievements. The higher I climb the better I see that the noble have no regard for the standard working hours of their world. They rise early and retire late. They work weekends. They only qualify for rest when the job is done. I was intrigued to learn from reliable sources that Bishop David Oyedepo works about sixteen hours in a day. Apparently, his day is not ended until he has read a new book, which is always waiting on his bedside table at bedtime. I never cease to be challenged by the tireless work ethics of one of my professional role model. This successful wife and mother of four obviously start work early and retires late by the time indicated on the email she sends me. It is no wonder that she carries as much clout as to be entrusted with the heavy responsibility of overhauling the entire London metropolis mental health services to bring them to par with contemporary standards.

Hard work does not kill it pays! There is no substitute to hard work. He who must achieve much must sacrifice much and he who must achieve little must sacrifice little. John Maxwell world authority on leadership said-No one can do the minimum and reach his maximum potential.

Achievers know how to choose hard work over a hard life. They not only work hard on their job but also on themselves. Rod Shoaff, twentieth century business guru was renowned to have said- "Work hard on your job and you make a living, work hard on yourself and you make a fortune". They work hard not just at delivering to but delighting their customers. They make a habit of under-promising and over-delivering. They act above and beyond the call of duty.

Winners work hard on themselves, their emotions, attitudes, reactions to adversity, and interpersonal skills. They recognise the synergy of teamwork and make personal sacrifices to keep their teams together.

Great men work on

It is the consistent, unrelenting application of appro-priate and commensurate effort that generates lasting success in any of life's endeavours. It has been said that it takes about ten thousand hours or the equivalence of seven years work to master your craft .History has proven time and again that the golden fleece of lasting achievement is reserved for men who work on despite the odds and temporary failures. The most natural response to opposition is quitting. Not so with the great.

No other event in history brings home this message to me more than the account of the gold search of the Darbys as recorded in Napoleon Hill's *Think and Grow Rich*. The Darbys left their hometown Williamsburg, Maryland and followed the gold-rush fever to Colorado where they began their digging for wealth. After several weeks of labour, they were rewarded with sighting of the precious ore ,which promised to fetch enough to clear their debts and make them a comfortable fortune.

The sample tests were promising they had found gold of sterling quality. However, disbelief turned into disappointment and then despair as they lost the gold vein following deeper search. They eventually gave up hope, sold their digging machinery cheaply to a junk man and returned home to Maryland worst than they left.

The junk man however enlisted the help of a mining engineer who advised him of the approximate spot to dig to relocate the gold vein. The predictions were accurate. The vein was rediscovered just three feet away from where the Darbys stopped their digging. The junkman made a fortune from the mine where the Darbys had expended several weeks of hard labour but gave up just before hitting their target. How many potential successful people have been robbed of the opportunity because they gave up too soon? I am an ardent hunter of success stories, and I am yet to find many who struck gold at their first attempt. It appears that success tends to hide itself reserved to be found by those who seek it hard enough to persevere in the face of apparent failure.

Great Men work smart

It is not enough to work hard. Effort creatively applied for long enough guarantees success quicker and easier. The cream of the crop in life's pursuit knows the secret of habitually refining their methods and techniques. Whether you are a pastor, professional or professor you must continually explore better methods of serving your clientele if you wish to remain relevant for long. Lasting winners are lifelong learners. They relentlessly ask how they can improve their service delivery.

I hold a firm conviction that the current global hostile economic climate is for the rise but fall of many. Creative workers are going to seize it as a stepping- stone to dizzy heights. It is time to think outside the box. Creative thinkers are leaders and creative thinking requires solitude and tranquillity. Step away from the problem to find its solution.

Great Men work with passion

Passion is simply emotional energy in motion. No one accomplishes much who is not passionate about his course. Ralph Emerson said "Nothing great has ever been accomplished without enthusiasm". Passion is enthusiasm with sustained corresponding action. If you wish to reach the pinnacle of your ladder, learn to climb up with passion.

In my view passion is as much a crucial ingredient to achieving success as sustaining it. You only need to take a look at the empires that have risen and fallen in history t convince yourself. Each one of them from the Roman to the Egyptian and Babylonian empires rose out of a passion to overcome adversity and fell at the time of plenty after they ran out of emotional steam.

It takes passion to get others to join your matter no matter your course. Late Dame Anita Roddick, the brain behind the Body Shop success story said- "You persuade people with passion, so you've got to have a product or service you feel emotionally charged about. Then you can tell stories about it that will inspire others".

Passion is palpable. It does not take a genius to tell whether you are merely paying lip service to your product-ministry, profession, family, business or career; or you are really passionate about it. Great men work with passion. If you persistently find it a job to muster passion in your endeavour, perhaps you need to be considering alternatives. Passion does not only propel you up the ladder, it keeps you on the pinnacle.

What the bible says about Diligence and Work

Small beginnings become great ends.

Job 8:6-7

If thou were pure and upright; surely now he would awake for thee, and make the habitation of thy righteousness prosperous.

Though thy beginning was small, yet thy latter end should greatly increase.

Results are for determined starters

Ecclesiastes 11:4

He that observes the wind shall not sow; and he that regards the clouds shall not reap.

Leadership and riches is acquired by diligence

Proverbs 10:4

He who has a slack hand becomes poor, but the hand of the diligent makes rich.

Proverbs 12:2

The hand of the diligent shall bear rule: but the slothful shall be under tribute.

Hastiness breeds lack

Proverbs 21:5

The thoughts of the diligent tend only to plenteousness; but of every one that is hasty only to want.

Consistent work is eventually rewarded with success

Galatians 6:9-10

And let us not grow weary while doing good, for in due season we shall reap if we do not lose heart. 10 Therefore, as we have opportunity, let us do good to all, especially to those who are of the household of faith.

Wisdom (creativity) is better than Strength (mere hard work)

Ecclesiastes 9:14-18

There was a little city with few men in it; and a great king came against it, besieged it, and built great snares around it. Now there was found in it a poor wise man, and he by his wisdom delivered the city. Then I said: "Wisdom is better than strength. Nevertheless, the poor man's wisdom is despised, and his words are not heard. Words of the wise, spoken quietly, should be heard. Rather than the shout of fools. Wisdom is better than weapons of war; but one sinner destroys much good."

Chapter Eight Summary

1. There is no substitute for diligence in the recipe for success.

2. Diligence is the art of being constant in the application of effort

3. Success is always a product of simple, consistent, planned, prepared and skilled discipline applied every day, compounded over time.

4. Great men start work, work hard, work on and work smart.

5. Every great project begins small. The first step to finishing is starting.

6. Achievers are self-motivated long and hard workers who choose hard work over a hard life.

7. Winners work hard on their jobs as well as on their emotions, attitudes, reactions and interpersonal skills.

8. History has always rewarded great men who work hard against odds and temporary set back and defeats.

9. Quicker and easier success is guaranteed by smarter creative work.

10. The bible teaches that

    a. Small endeavours are precursors of great ones

    b. Results are reserved for those who start work

    c. Leadership and riches is acquired by diligence

    d. Hastiness breeds lack

    e. Consistent work is eventually rewarded with success

    f. Wisdom is better than strength.

Action Plan and reflections

1. What one project or endeavour do you need to start? Write down what action you would take today, in the next seven days and one month to start this great work.

2. In all sincerity, ask yourself whether you are giving your best to your current most pressing life pursuit. It could be your marriage, children, ministry or career.

3. What is the weapon of discouragement that is most effective against your pursuit? List two strategies you would adopt to ensure consistency to accomplishment in the future.

4. List two strategies of creativity you would adopt in the life pursuit identified in 2 above. Then write down when you would begin to use the strategy and when you would evaluate your progress.

If your success begins and ends with you, it's a failure in disguise-

Bishop David Oyedepo

The short cut to success is to find somebody who is doing what you want to do, and study and duplicate their actions without changing the principles. Then you will achieve the same results

-Ancient Greek maxim.

CHAPTER 9

Dissemination Habit of Giants

A successful person, system or institution without a successor is an utter and pitiable failure. What is the point in paying a dear price to get to the pinnacle of your life's pursuit if there is no one to propagate the work at your demise? If you are the leader of a family, church, business or institution that only works well when you are present then you have cause to be concerned.

One of the secrets of exponentially increasing your impact is to replicate or disseminate your values in others. In order for their life's work to live on after them, great men make a planned and concerted effort to nurture and mentor others to follow their footprints. Look out for the sequel book to the *Footprints of Giants* where my memos on mentoring would be published.

Jesus was a great mentor. He asked his disciples to follow him and expect the natural consequence of becoming fishers of men like he was. He devoted a remarkable portion of his apparently short three -year earthly ministry to teaching his inner core course the deep secrets of the kingdom. No wonder despite his relatively short stay with them, his teachings live on and as strong twenty- one centuries on.

Let me ask you, are you so busy maintaining your high status that you are neglecting the crucial role of teaching others to rise? One way to guarantee lasting achievement is to show others how to achieve. It is more rewarding not just to be a success story but be part of the success story of many others. Benjamin Disreali, nineteenth century English Prime Minister, statesman and poet said- *The greatest good you can do for others is not just to share your riches but to reveal to him his own.*

History has shown that most celebrated winner's encountered heart breaking obstacles before they triumphed. They won because they refused to become discouraged by their defeats (Harvey Mackay). And, thankfully, a great number of them kept the records of their trials and triumph for the sake of posterity. It has been said that a life worth living is a life worth recording.

Let me introduce you to the common and relatively easily imbibed habit of journaling practised by achievers. I have found out that many great men both of old and in the present keep journals. They take a serious and usually daily approach to recording the lessons they learn as they climb up the ladder and pass these on to their protégés.

I discovered the joy and benefits of journaling whilst trying to kill the boredom of an inpatient hospital stay several years ago. I have since then been erratic and inconsistent in my efforts. However, compiling the manuscript of this book has kept me more focussed and I dare say I am the better for it. Journaling is simply the act of periodically recording one's thoughts, inspirations, spiritual lessons and life experiences in a safe accessible medium. It may contain a powerful quote, a revelation from personal devotion or inspiration from a book read or a message heard. It could be the receptacle to hold and preserve the delights and milestones of today and the tasks for tomorrow. Journals differ from a diary, which is strictly used to keep appointments and important events without the lessons derived from them.

Journaling has various other benefits in addition to being a mentoring tool. I have found them useful in :

1. Recording divine instructions and inspirations

It has been said that a blunt pen is sharper than a sharp memory. I have discovered from journaling that writing down divine instructions helps you execute them quicker and faster. There is a force in writing which brings intangible concepts into the realm of reality.

2. *Encouraging meditation*

Journaling forces your mind to focus. The act of writing motivates the subject to contemplate and ruminate. Meditation has its benefits. It generates inspiration from thoughts and events like ruminant animals derive nutrients from chewing their curd.

3. Refining my thoughts

The best way to come up with a really good idea is to come up with a lot of ideas (Linus Pauling, Nobel prize winning scientist). The act of writing down thoughts supports the process of refining and making them clearer.

4. Observing and learning from recurring patterns

5. Preserving ideas and inspiration

The words below sums up this benefit of journaling-

> *I suppose that every old scholar has had the experience of reading something in a book which has significance to him, but which he could never find again. Sure he is, that he read it there, but no one else ever read it nor can he find it again, though he buy the book and ransack every page. How true! What we do not somehow capture today is lost forever. There are lot of things in life*

we can trust, but my experience in life has taught me that the human memory is definitely not one of them (Emerson).

It is for this reason that it is crucial to quote in an easily retrievable manner the source of quotes or inspirations verbatim to the page and paragraph of source when journaling. The habit of dating and recording venue also preserves the experience in his context.

6 .Encouraging personal accountability

There is a power in recording thoughts that keeps one accountable. A review of personal journal is always a reminder to focus on the things that matter in life. Every human life must have a ultimate focus, which should be to please its creator. Pleasing God equates to fulfilling to the letter what each human was born to be. I find the experience of journaling helpful in keeping me committed to being who I was born to be.

Effective Journaling

One may wonder at the onset where to begin or what to write in a journal. You would however discover that no sooner than you begin to capture and record your thoughts, life experiences and resultant lessons, that you find there is more than enough for each day. It is not only the joys and victories of life that should be recorded but also the challenging detoured courses travelled to obtain them. Journals can also be safes for keeping the precious goals and aspirations for the future; and landmark the milestones to achieving them. Here are a few crucial helpful personal observations for intending beginners.

1. Start memorable

Choose a milestone date such as a birthday, anniversary, New Year day or a date of note to begin. The memorable date does not have to be a previously recognised one. A Chinese proverb says the best time to plant a tree was twenty years ago, the second best time is today. Today could become memorable by your decision to commence journaling as a result of reading these notes.

2. Record verbatim

It is helpful for posterity to form a pattern of recording dates, context and sources of entries as verbatim as possible. I find that quoting the source helps for ease of reference in the future. It could be frustrating to wish to cite a quote or story in a sermon, but end up spending countless precious hours trying to find its original source.

3. Journal to pattern

The first step after the decision to commence journaling is to obtain a medium-book or electronic pad you are comfortable with. It is important to carefully choose your medium being mindful of its requirement for longevity and durability. I find it helpful to habitually carry a pen and post it stickers in which I record as soon as possible with a view to eventually transfer into the main journal. It is beneficial to form a habit of having a pen and paper always within easy reach. You can never tell when a life changing monumental moment or inspiration would occur.

The next step is to develop a pattern by recurrent practise, which evolves into a profitable habit. A daily recording would generate more material than a weekly or monthly routine. Some may however find it easier to build up to a more regular routine over time. A smart use of time would be to incorporate journaling into already established devotional time where writing is included. Bill Hybel best selling author of *Too Busy to Pray* advocates writing out prayer during devotion.

4. Create Time

Forming the habit of stepping away from the hustle and bustle of life to be alone with God creates a preponderance of "journallable" moments and events. It is expedient to plan regular periods of retreat into your annual calendar right from the onset. One of my goals for the future is to be able to spend a weekend each quarter in a time of spiritual solitude.

5. Review entries

Bob Burg in his ebook *The Success Formula* said "knowledge without action is same as having no knowledge at all". What is the point in capturing such life changing lessons and keeping them locked up in a journal? A habitual periodical review of journals keeps the lessons alive and accessible for action, which liberates the transforming potential of the experience.

What the bible teaches abut Dissemination

Jesus himself was a great mentor

Matthew 4:19

Follow me and I would make you fishers of men

Mentoring is encouraged in society

1 Timothy 4:12

Let no man despise your youth but be thou an example of believers in word, in conversation, in charity, in spirit, in faith, in purity.

Mentoring should be taught

Titus 2:3-5

The aged women likewise, that they be in behaviour as becometh holiness, not false accusers , not given to much wine, teachers of good things;

That they may teach the young women to be sober, to love their husbands and to love their children, To be discreet, chaste, keepers at home, good, obedient to their own husbands, that the word of God be not blasphemed.

People should use time with discretion

Psalms 90:12

So, teach us to number our days that we may apply our hearts unto wisdom.

God instructed Journaling

Habakkuk 2:2-3

And the Lord answered me, and said Write the vision and make it plain upon tables, that he may run that readeth it.

For the vision is yet for an appointed time, but at the end it shall speak, and not lie,: though it tarry wait for it; because it will surely com,e it will not tarry

Chapter Nine Summary

1. A success story without a successor is an utter and pitiable failure.

2. One of the secrets of multiplying ones influence many folds is to replicate and disseminate ones values in others via mentoring.

3. Jesus was a great mentor, hence despite a relatively short earthly ministry; He has a lasting and growing influence till date.

4. The greatest good you can do for others is not just to share your riches but to reveal to him his own.

5. Most celebrated world achievers recorded their trials and triumphs for posterity.

6. A life worth living is a life worth recording.

7. Journal keeping is a common and easily imbibed habit of achievers.

8. Journaling is the act of periodically recording one's thoughts, inspirations, spiritual lessons and life experiences in a safe accessible medium. Journals are more than diaries, which are exclusively used to keep appointments and important dates, without the lessons derived from them.

9. The benefits of journaling include

    9.1   Encouraging meditation

    9.2   Refining thought processes

    9.3   Observing and learning from
           recurring patterns

    9.4   Preservation of ideas and inspirations
           and their sources

    9.5   Encouraging personal accountability

10. Tips on keeping a effective journal are

    10.1   start on a memorable occasion

    10.2   Record journal content verbatim

    10.3   Journal in a recurring pattern

    10.4   Create journaling time

    10.5   Review journal entries periodically

11. What the bible says about dissemination

    11.1   Jesus was a great mentor

    11.2   Bible encourages mentoring

    11.3   Mentoring should be taught

    11.4   People should use time with
            discretion

    11.5   God instructed Journaling

Reflections and Action Plan

1. Choose an area of your life where you would like to increase your influence by mentoring others

2. Prayerfully seek out one or two mentees whose lives you intend to influence to release their full potential.

3. Set a date when you would begin your journaling.

4. Confide in a trusted friend your plans in 1-3 above and obtain a journal within the next week.

Success is not final, failure is not fatal; it is the courage to continue that counts.

Sir Winston Churchill Former British Prime Minister

Whenever I have faced a set back, I have dusted myself down and got on with the rest of my life because I believed in myself.

Sir Philip Green, UK Retail Billionaire

The true means of being misled is to believe oneself finer than the others.

Francois Duc de la Rochefoucauld, Seventeenth Century French author & writer

CHAPTER *10*

Demise of Giants

A ll humans were born giants, many may know it, some know how to manifest greatness, few live as such, but alas; even fewer remain giants long enough to leave a mark on time! This was my opening sentence and as I conclude, I would like to take you back to basics.

Let me share with you a sobering but true story I have come across from multiple sources in my study of the great. In 1923, there was a convention in a Chicago hotel of the nine wealthiest men in the world. Their combined wealth was more than that of the United States Treasury. Among these elite group was the then president of the largest private steel industry, Charles Schwab. Others were Arthur Ceutten , greatest Wheat speculator, Jesse Livermore the greatest bear on the Wall street and Ivar Krueger, head of World's greatest monopoly. The group was completed by Samuel Insull largest electric utility company president, Howard Hopson, president of largest gas company and President of New York Stock exchange, Richard Whitney. The other two were Leon Fraser President of the bank of international settlements and Albert Fall, a prominent member of President Harding's cabinet.

Each of these men ended up as giants who did not maintain their status for long enough to pass it on or leave a lasting mark on their time. Twenty- five years on three of them had died by suicide, two died in a foreign land financially bankrupt, two had served jail sentences and one had lost his mind.

So whatever befell the giants that became living monuments of dead successes? Their relics remain as prominent pointers of faded glory. Where did it all go wrong? Up today and down tomorrow. Why does it seem like it's easier to achieve than sustain success? Where are the sons of yesterday's giants? What has stolen away the future of the princes of past noble kings? Indeed many it seems achieve greatness but very few perpetuate it to coming generations.

The truth, my dear reader, is that the crown does not automatically endure through generations. There are attitudes and habits potent enough to slay even the greatest of giants. And you better know and rid yourself of such killers because they never fail to accomplish their destructive mission each time. And as sure as the vultures find carcasses these giant slayers are attracted by a noble and great life.

Arrogance

The scripture warns that pride always ends up in a fall. Arrogance and a sense of self- sufficiency is an inevitable and on going temptation for the achiever. As sure as it comes so is its guarantee to slay its victim if allowed to linger.

Arrogant men and women are on a self destructive mission. If you are enjoying a cruise up your ladder, save yourself a mighty fall by brutally eliminating any thoughts of invincibility. Do yourself the favour of keeping friends and keepsakes that remind you of where and how you started! Be ever alert that there is nothing that you possess that was not bestowed upon you. All we are and have are gifts from God. What have you got that was not bestowed on you? Remember your unique talents and skills may have created a way for you but only because there was an opportunity to express them. Opportunities are divinely granted.

Joseph, the dreamer had an unparalleled gift of dream interpretation and governance, but he could have died in prison but for the divine opportunity to appear in the palace.

No one should ever boast of their talents because they are divinely endowed investments. An investment is a deposit you have been entrusted with to generate further profit. The capital is not yours at the end of the day. You must also remember that you did not choose your talents or natural gifting. No man ever chooses their parents, race, social or spiritual background at birth.

Here are a few warning signs to look out for and eliminate promptly. Arrogance always starts in the thought realm. When one begins to feel superior to others and treat them with disdain as a result, it is time to be cautious. When your title, office or achievements becomes your defining factor, beware! It is time to prune yourself to size when you begin to look down on your superiors because you feel you are now at par with them. The same is true when you treat subordinates with disdain because you feel they would never measure up to you.

We must all strive to maintain a healthy self -worth and self -confidence but never get arrogant or pompous about your achievement. The giants who keep the status long enough to pass it on to generations are the humblest of men. Arrogance is a destiny killer. Kill it before it kills you!

The rationale question to ask is how do you eliminate pride? I have heard religious people pray that God should humble them, but if the scriptural records of those God humbled is examined, it is easy to see the folly of this prayer. Do you remember the Babylonian king who was relegated to communion with beasts when God humbled him? How about the proverbial rich fool in Jesus' parable whose life was required of him the same day he boasted of his self -sufficiency?

The bible teaches that it is your responsibility to humble yourself. You need to prune yourself to size by exerting discipline in your thoughts about how you think of yourself relative to others. What in the nifty gritty determines your worth when the chips are down? The bottom line is that arrogance always starts from the thought realm. It is simply put, thinking of yourself more highly than you ought. The remedy is to accept your folly and fine tune the thermostat of your self worth. Waiting for an event or others to cut you to size is always a humiliating experience. Save yourself the shame.

Bitterness

American Television News broadcaster David Brinkley, who became one of America's most well known and beloved news personalities, said "A successful man is one who can lay a firm foundation with the bricks others have thrown at him". How true! Brinkley's words reminded me of an African adage that says; only the ripe fruits are aimed at by the harvesters sickle.

I am happy to be the bearer of glad tidings that your achievement would attract criticism. No one ever does anything worthwhile without being criticised. The greater news is you have a choice of response.

You could choose to see criticism as a brick to be thrown back at distracters engendering strife and bitterness; or a material for building a firm resilient character. I chose the later. Criticisms are helpful because they allow you to perform a reality check on your values, standards, motives and outcomes. However ,you must not focus on them. It has been said that if you take to heart and dwell on every criticism you encounter you would never travel far in your life's journey.

Be brutally truthful in your analysis, change if there is a genuine reason to do so, but never allow criticism to fester bitterness and ill feeling towards critics or stop you in your tracks.

A man who must travel far must travel light. Bitterness and bad will towards critics is an emotional weight you do not want to carry if you are headed for the top of the ladder. A man who has others bound with threads of un-forgiveness has in essence bound himself in chains and cables of limitations. Criticism could make you bitter or better, the call is yours.

Complacency

Complacency is a state of false satisfaction and accomplishment that negates further aspirations. No matter how great your accomplishment there is always a room for improvement. There are more charities to be endowed, more souls to be saved, and more frontiers to be reached with your life's mission. No one must rest on their oars until they breathe their last. I could not agree more with Ray Crocs, brain behind the McDonald franchise empire who said you grow as long as you remain green.

Complacency sends into a deep sleep and initiates regression. There is a land called more. Keep your passion alive. Passion is sustained based on perpetual exposure to new opportunities. Consciously expose yourself to new experiences for the benefit of searching out opportunities to make impact. Visit new countries, take a new course, learn a new language, do whatever it takes to keep aglow your passion to harness every minute of time and resources doing what you were born to do.

Abraham Lincoln said when you stop learning you are old, whether you are twenty or eighty. When you stop learning, you start dying-Dr T L Osborn. How many achievers have blighted their progress when they awarded themselves a well done too soon? And Rev Dr

Paul Jinadu said " *my idea of a clever man is one who never stops learning*". Keep your passion and your life!

Discouragement

I do not cease to be amazed when I hear the inside intimate stories of the discouragement some of my role models and mentors have contended with and overcome. One tends to be fooled into the fallacy of concluding they are without the struggles of despondency when you behold the giants' all together well turned out performance on the stage of life. Alas, I have come to conclude that season of despair are common to all- the great and small, young and old, noble and ignoble, rich and poor, righteous and unrighteous.

In fact, I am yet to come across any noble person of repute who does not have a story of overcoming discouragement. What however determines whether they emerge victorious or not is the choices they make at this low season. You need to have at hand a ready- made remedy for discouragement when; not if it comes, as it would certainly come.

Allow me to wear my psychiatric and pastoral caps as I share a few proven remedies.

1. Realise that you are not peculiar in your battle against despondency.

2. Seek God as your ultimate source of help.

3. Revisit and review the personal promises God has made to you in the past.

4. Indulge in activities that naturally lift your mood even if you find them mechanical initially. I find listening to worship music, Christian inspirational messages and long solitary prayer walks helpful at such times.

5. Make a choice to focus your thoughts on achievements rather than setbacks. This would take discipline and effort as the natural tendency at periods of despondency is for the mind to filter out positive in preference for negative thoughts.

    There is ample research evidence showing that you can change the way you feel by consciously changing what you ruminate on.

6. Learn to seek the support and encouragement of trusted circle of confidants.

7. Develop a self-encouraging profile for seasons when your support system is unavailable or ineffective. You cannot always bank on others encouraging you always. Learn to encourage yourself!

Envy

Envy is the feelings of resentment towards others on account of their achievement or advantage. It is akin to an emotional cancerous condition that progressively takes over and destroys other cells in the mind. It genders other vices such as arrogance, lust, strife and unhealthy rivalry.

How many times have you heard about a fall from grace to grass story after the subject began to indulge in an unhealthy rivalry, which took over their focus, distracted from their main mission and ended in their demise. The biblical King Saul readily comes to mind. His rivalry of David, the Shepherd musical boy led to his inglorious death and succession by David.

Envy is lethal. Rid yourself of it by a reminder that no one is without divine endowment. You may look down on your assets but there are people who crave the very thing you devalue. Choose to extinguish envy from your thought processes.

We must always remember that our choices determine our chances in life. If you do not like your current life chances, you need to review your previous choices rather than envy your prosperous neighbour.

Fatal Failures / Setbacks

One who must maintain a sustained achievement must learn to overcome personal setbacks and failures. These unpleasant events may either be used as a motivation for further success or an excuse for quitting. The choice is always yours. Sir Winston Churchill English Prime Minister said Success is not final, failure is not fatal, but it is the courage to continue that counts. It is this courage to continue in the face of apparent defeat and failure that makes out winners from losers. Let me say this to you, do you know that every one who is a winner today is an ex-loser who got fed up of losing, enough to learn and master the techniques of winning?

It has been said that success does not consist in never making a blunder but in never making the same one a second time. (Josh Billings). Everyone errs in life but the victory lies in learning from the event no matter how costly and moving on regardless. Resolve this moment not to allow your failure to become fatal, rise above that set back and become a resounding fight-back success story!

It was intriguing to learn from folklore that the brain behind FedEx (Federal Express) had been awarded a C grade by his Yale University economics Professor for his paper on an overnight delivery system in a computer information age. The reason for the poor grade was that it was not a feasible concept. "Why would anyone want their parcels to arrive overnight?" quizzed the don.

Fredrick W Smith went ahead any way, to translate to his paper project into practise when the first overnight express delivery company in the world and largest in the United States was founded in 1971, five years after graduation. FedEx's total equity of $14.5 billion and employee strength of nearly three hundred thousand attests to the success that would result when a man confronts initial setback and apparent failure head on. Are you confronting or condoning your own setbacks?

It has been said that out of every adversity comes an equal or greater opportunity. The story of the history of artificial green tuft as told by Glenn Bland in his Success book, named after him proves this assertion. Apparently, the man -made tuft was conceived to avert a disaster after the playing field in an ultra modern sports arena built with a glass roof to shield adverse climatic conditions; failed to grow natural grass. The architects of this first of it's kind sports complex in Houston Texas went back to the drawing board and came up with the solution of man-made tuft, that was deemed superior to natural grass.

Gluttony & Greed

Stephen Covey in his *Seven Habits of Highly Effective People* warned that- "Before you start scrambling up the ladder of success make sure it is leaning against the right building". Stop for a moment to ask yourself what the true and deeply seated motivation for your success is. What point are you trying to prove? For some it is retaliation on perceived foes, others are driven by a fear of failure, and some wish to succeed to compensate for a loss or deprivation from the past hence they never seem to have enough no matter how much is amassed. An inordinate or wrong desire to amass possession or achieve success (covetousness) is itself destructive.

Believe me when I tell you that any other motivation for achievement other than to realise the full potential of who God created you to be and to become a great and profitable steward of your lifetime would always end in a deep sense of dissatisfaction.

The remedy to gluttony is to admit it and habitually indulge in sacrificial giving. How about starting with taking a look at your wardrobe and giving away to charity or the less privileged all garments you have not worn in two years. There is a liberating power in giving to the poor that takes away the focus from your needs to those of others. In the final analysis, gluttony is rooted in selfishness.

Watch out for these seven giant killers. Kill them before they kill you if you wish to enjoy a long peaceful reign as the giant you were born to be.

What the bible says about the slayer of giants.

Greatness is not automatically perpetuated

Proverbs 27:23-4

Be diligent to know the state of thy flocks, and look well to thy herds. For riches are not forever: and doth the crown endure to every generation?

God hates Pride and arrogance

Proverbs 6:16-17

These six things doth the Lord hate, yea, seven are an abomination unto him: A proud look, a lying tongue, and hands that shed innocent blood

Pride (arrogance) always heralds destruction

Proverbs 16:18

Pride goeth before destruction and a haughty spirit before a fall.

Bitterness breeds trouble

Hebrews12:15

Looking diligently lest any man fail of the grace of God; lest any root of bitterness springing up trouble you, and thereby many be defiled

Ephesians 4:31

Let all bitterness, and wrath, and anger, and clamour, and evil speaking, be put away from you, with all malice.

Slackness (complacency) births poverty

Proverbs 10:4-

He becometh poor that dealeth with a slack hand, but the hand of the diligent maketh rich.

Proverbs 20:13

Love not lest thou come to poverty, open thy eyes and thou shall be satisfied with bread.

Slothfulness wastes great potential

Proverbs 18:9

He also that is slothful in his work is brother to him that is a great waster.

Persistence has rewards

Galatians 6:9-10

And let us not be weary in well doing: for in due season we shall reap, if we faint not. As we therefore opportunity , let us do good unto all men, especially unto them who are of the household of faith.

Envy has consequences

Proverbs 14:30 (Amplified bible)

A calm and undisturbed mind and heart are the life and health of the body, but envy, jealousy, and wrath are like rottenness of the bones.

Falling is not fatal or final for the righteous

Psalms 145:14

The Lord upholdeth all that fall, and raises up all that be bowed down.

Proverbs 24:16

For the righteous man falleth seven times and rises up again

Greed equates to self destruction

Proverbs 15:27

He that is greedy of gain troubleth his own house: but he that hateth gifts shall live.

Gluttony results in poverty

Proverbs 23:21

For the drunkard and glutton shall come to poverty and drunkenness shall clothe a man with rags.

Chapter Ten Summary

1. Every human being was born programmed and destined to live a profound life with lasting legacy.

2. Many men started well but finished pitiably in life's journey and pursuits.

3. There are killer attitudes and habits that destroy potential and destiny.

4. Arrogance is self- destructive. Achievers must remain humble to maintain their status.

5. Arrogance begins with a thought of invincibility.

6. Giants have a personal responsibility to remain humble.

7. Success inevitably attracts criticism, but the successful have a choice to either be bitter or better from critics.

8. Complacency results in regression. It occurs when passion for novelty is lost.

9. Life long learning protects against complacency.

10. Discouragement is a common temptation to all, irrespective of socioeconomic status.

11. Achievers need to master the art of overcoming discouragement. There are proven remedies for this.

12. Envy genders other unhealthy attitudes and habits.

13. It distracts an achievers focus, and could terminate their mission.

14. Our choices in life determine our chances.

15. Failure and setbacks are not inevitably fatal, but could be used as an incentive for a fight-back success.

16. The only satisfying and lasting motivation for success is to be nothing short of who God made you to be.

17. Greed and gluttony are destiny slayers, but they can be avoided.

18. The bible teaches that

    18.1   Greatness is not spontaneously propagated to generations.

    18.2   God hates pride and arrogance.

    18.3   Arrogance heralds destruction.

    18.4   Bitterness breeds trouble.

18.5   Slackness makes poor and
       wastes potentials.

18.6   Persisting courage has rewards.

18.7   Envy has consequences.

18.8   Falling does not have to be fatal for the
       righteous.

18.9   Greed equates to self destruction

18.10 Gluttony results in poverty.

Philippians 2: 9-11

Wherefore God also hath highly exalted him (Jesus) and given him a name that is above every name: 10 That at the name of Jesus very knee should bow, of things in heaven, and things in earth and things under the earth; And that every tongue should confess that Jesus Christ is Lord to the glory of God the Father.

Acts 4:12

Neither is there salvation in any other: for there is none other name under heaven given among men whereby we must be saved.

CHAPTER 11

Giant of all Giants

A llow me to introduce to you the giant of all giants. He is the all time giant. It is by Him that all things that exist were made. There is no genuine or lasting life or achievement outside of Him. He is the King of Kings and Lord of Lords. He lived a short life of thirty- three years two hundred centuries ago but the legacy of a great, immaculate and selfless life giving life lives on.

I am talking about Jesus the Christ, the author of life. He is life personified and the embodiment of God (His father's) glory. He is the source of true wisdom and master of the universe. He is the governor among the nations and the soon coming king of Israel. He is the Lion of Judah and the Rod of Jesse.

Kings have come and gone, empires have risen and fallen, but His kingdom remains eternally untarnished, vibrant and flourishing. There is no ceasing to His everlasting kingdom because it is founded on righteousness and justice. He reigns forever and ever.

Jesus is greatness itself. He is the only one who can make a man truly great by leading them to the purpose for which He made them. He directs by His Holy Spirit to the people a man has been called to serve. There is really no true greatness outside of Christ. Attempting to achieve lasting and fulfilling success without Him is like swimming up the Niagara Falls.

Jesus who died and rose again thereby breaking the power of death and hell is the only one who can by His Spirit reveal success bursting habits. By the same power of resurrection He confers, we can now break those habits and form life- propagating ones.

The author of life who gives the water that makes a man to never thirst again is the conferrer of a desire to live a full and fulfilling life. He works in His creation to will (desire) and do His good pleasure which He has ordained for us before the world's foundation. The desire for true greatness serving those to whom you were appointed, is from Christ, the one who came to serve and save sinners.

There is no true development until the spirit of man is made alive and reconciled back to his creator. It is then the soul may acquire knowledge and appropriately use this information to it's advantage via communication from the Holy Spirit. The true Rabbi is the one who allows a man to flourish in his spirit, soul and body.

How many times do you come across people who have good intentions but never seem to be able to discipline themselves to execute them? Jesus by his self -denial at the cross of Calvary where he laid down His life for mankind became the epitome of a disciplined life. He is the only one who can confer the ability to maintain discipline in your thought, talk, timing and tranquillity. The precious Lamb of God is the King who allows you to appreciate your own worth and value in Him. He reveals to you by His spirit your strengths and helps you to overcome your weaknesses by making available His own strength.

Jesus the friend that sticks closer than a brother has the omniscience to lead you into associations and relationships that would enrich your life and allow you to maximise your destiny. With the great Teacher in your life and His spirit leading you into all truth, you would be empowered to make right choices that count for eternity.

The great Shepherd of the Sheep is the true mentor who makes a great mentor and mentee out of even the most inexperienced. He is the one that leads into the green pastures of life and leads a man to his wealthy places. The secret of the wealth of hidden places and treasures of dark places are plain to him. This benevolent and gracious king is the one clothes a man with irresistible favour that brings him into the palace of kings.

The captain of my salvation specialises in making winners out of losers and victors out of victims. He is the changer of stories, my glory and the lifter up of my head. The sinless Lamb of God is the one who empowers a man to avoid the destiny killers of arrogance, bitterness, complacency and discouragement.

I make no reservation in declaring boldly that Jesus is the secret of my achievements. He made me whatever I am now and aspire to be. My life would not be as attractive as it is without His saving grace and His generous giving of His Spirit to reside in my heart and giving me directions day by day. What would my life have been like without Him. He is my succour, my helper, my strong tower and deliverer. He lifts up my head.

If you have not experienced a personal relationship with Jesus, I invite you to do so this moment. It is as simple as acknowledging you are not able to please God of your own accord no matter who hard you try. Admit you are a sinner by nature and ask him to forgive your sins and make you new.

Invite Jesus into your life to take control and be your Lord. Then find a Bible believing Church where the word of God is preached to attend regularly. Begin to study the bible where you would discover and develop the path to true greatness here on earth and later in heaven.

Liberty

Let me share with you news of an extraordinary piece of work that I am involved in. I am a medical volunteer with Liberty, a Christian Charity that has in the last ten years been nurturing and releasing giants in the rural unreached villages of Africa via agricultural empowerment, free education, pastoral care, provision of portable water and free health services.

Liberty's vision is to reach African villages so that communities may be transformed body, soul and mind – that communities have access to basic amenities in order to live healthy lives and fulfil their destiny in God. We believe that through the love of God and support of our sponsors together we can eradicate poverty and raise a new generation of leaders in Africa.

There are various ways you can directly or indirectly support this vision.

Become a Fundraiser

There are several methods to raise funds from a single donation to regular donations, running a marathon, walking the Great Wall of China or setting up a stall at your school fete. You could even ask employers to consider matching the money you raise.

Some fundraisers have asked guests at their celebrations-birthdays, weddings to make a donation to Liberty as alternative to giving gifts.

Shares- giving is a tax saving method of giving one may wish to consider. You could also donate royalties or proceeds from a book, work of art or intellectual property.

To set up your own fundraising page for the charity and get your friends to donate please visit:

www.justgiving.com/liberty

Become a Volunteer

You may consider coming out with us on our annual autumn village outreach trips to Africa to gain a first hand experience of the work. I am yet to find anyone who did not find the experience life transforming.

Sponsor a Child, Teacher or Well

May I encourage you to visit our website and learn how you could sponsor a child, a teacher, a well or a cataract operation. You may wish to make contact with us via the details below

Liberty

21-29 Pendennis street

London

SW16 2SS

Telephone: +44 0208 688 2814

E-mail: Liberty4nations@gmail.com

www.makingpeoplefree.org.uk

First Steps in Greatness

Mortimer Adler in his book *How to Read a Book said In the case of good books, the point is not to see how many of them you can get through, but how many can get through to you.* I am hopeful that indeed reading this book has left indelible marks on your life. It however does not stop at acknowledging the beauty of the work. In what way is your life and those of others around you going to change as a result of your reading this book?

I encourage you to return to my opening suggestions on how one could turn good intentions to practical habits and decide what you are going to do with what you have read. It is always helpful not to try fulfilling your promise to yourself alone but to make yourself accountable to a trusted buddy who can perk you up when your enthusiasm and motivation runs low.

I want to conclude by reaffirming that you can be the giant you were born to be. Begin to take those steps today.

If this book has blessed you in any way or form you can pay that blessing forward by recommending it to a friend, loaning out your own copy or buying one for them. Be a Giant and disseminate the seeds of greatness you picked up in this book.

Look out for the sequel to the Footprint of Giants.

Thank you for reading and God bless you.

Live the great Life!